THE LEGEND OF

BRUCE LEE

Alex Ben Block

A DELL BOOK

Published by
Dell Publishing Co., Inc.
1 Dag Hammarskjold Plaza
New York, New York 10017

Dell ® TM 681510, Dell Publishing Co., Inc.
Printed in the United States of America
First printing—March 1974
Second printing—May 1974
Third printing—June 1974

KING OF KUNG FU

His unique mastery of the martial arts put his personal stamp on this most ancient of traditions as he shared with the world what once had been the exclusive property of the privileged few.

His larger-than-life energies, appetites, ambitions and genius filled his career with glory, scandal, rumor and controversy—from his earliest appearances in public to his strange and shocking death.

The movies he made have become classics of their kind, destined to stand forever as supreme presentations of Kung Fu.

Whatever he did, whatever he said, however he acted in public and in private, there has never been anyone quite like him, and there is no one who can replace him.

In death, as in life, Bruce Lee remains the King of Kung Fu—and here for the first time is his incredible story.

Tony C.

"A martial artist is a human being first. Just as nationalities have nothing to do with one's humanity, so they have nothing to do with the martial arts."

"Life is a constant process of relating."

"Man, the living creature, the creating individual, is always more important than any established style."

BRUCE LEE SIU LOONG
THE LITTLE DRAGON

November 27, 1940
San Francisco

July 20, 1973
Hong Kong

To Fanny Polivan who taught me
the only two things in life I'd ever truly need,
Canasta and Poker.

Contents

THE LEGEND OF BRUCE LEE

Introduction

"The summer insect will not know what ice is; the frog in the well will not realize the immensity of the sky."
"He who has seen little marvels much."
"If you see something strange and ignore it, its strangeness will vanish."

— CHINESE PROVERBS

What do Ryan O'Neal, Elvis Presley, Raymond St. Jacques, Steve McQueen, James Caan, Fred Williamson, Angela Mao, Larry Hagman, Buddy Rich, Tim Considine, Dennis Hopper, Peter Fonda, Herb Albert, Peggy Lipton, John Saxon, Dick Martin, Robert Goulet, Mike Connors, Sterling Silliphant, Ron "Tarzan" Ely, James Coburn, Bruce Lee and Gracie Slick have in common?

They are all martial artists.

They keep the faith not at incensed temples, but at sweat-stinking dojos where hundreds of thousands of Americans in baggy white gis yell and grunt through kata, kumite, motions and emotions that make up the disciplined life of the martial artist.

They study the ancient Eastern arts of kung fu, aikido, judo or karate among more than forty styles of martial arts practiced in the U.S. alone, or hundreds more practiced in Asia.

Some, like Presley or Williamson, practice daily, while others have digested the basics and train when they find the time.

Why? What attracted these celebrities and numerous other young men and women to the dojos that have sprung up in cities and towns in the past few years? Is there a common appeal?

And what about the extraordinary boom in films featuring the martial arts? Or the phenomenal success of the television show "Kung Fu"? Is this just a fad or a full-scale Oriental invasion? Who are the stars of the martial arts, and where have they come from?

Many answers begin to emerge as this book focuses on the greatest of all the martial arts stars, the one whom all others will be compared with for all time, the late Bruce Lee.

What enthusiasts might agree they have in common is a need to find their own truth, and at its best, that is the true lesson of the martial arts.

"Liberating truth," said sensei (meaning teacher) Bruce Lee, "is a reality only in so far as it is *experienced and lived* by the individual himself; it is a truth that transcends styles or disciplines."

"Avert thy face from world deceptions, mistrust thy senses, they are false," teach the Buddhists. "But within thy body, the shrine of thy sensations, seek in the impersonal for the Eternal Man, and having sought him out, look inward; thou art Buddha."

Of course, the screaming kids who stream out of movie houses after an action-packed martial arts film aren't looking inward. They are reacting to a two-hour force feeding of cinematic violence, with unpredictable results.

It was Bruce Lee's ability, on screen and off, to cross this gap between Zen intent and violent result that made him truly special. He was a great fighter and an interesting human being who knew how to communicate to both East and West.

His films marked the high point of the wave of martial arts films, just as surely as his death dooms this flood to recede in time.

Bruce Lee lived and flourished on life's electric fringe. He had a Napoleonic sense of his own potency and worshipped instinctual energy.

He had two great passions, show business and his personal style of Chinese karate, Jeet Kune Do, in essence a sophisticated form of street fighting.

He expressed his passions in movie-making, love-making, money-making and training. He arrived as suddenly as a sleek race car turning a corner and smashed against the far wall.

He will be remembered as a footnote to history for a number of reasons. He was the first Chinese-American to reach worldwide superstar status. In the West, for many, his name and legend are irrevocably interwoven with the idea of martial arts, and in legend he lives on as their champion. He introduced the flourishing Hong Kong film industry to international audiences and paved the way for a spate of imitators. And perhaps most importantly he entered and made his mark in history with impeccable timing.

If Mao hadn't brought China together, if Nixon hadn't gone there, if acupuncture's time hadn't come, if mysticism weren't in revival, if martial arts weren't an answer to crime in the streets, if kung fu didn't fill such an obvious void for a physical culture with socio-religious overtones, Bruce Lee might never have gotten beyond the Mandarin film circuit in South Asia. But the time had come and he was ready.

Bruce Lee had style, charisma and that magic of timing. There's no substitute for being in the right place at the right time, or for knowing how to make an audience desire as you withhold, until suddenly you ultra-deliver with wham-bam eye-boggling style.

This book is the story of Bruce Lee, the Hong Kong film industry he revolutionized, and his part in moving the West a giant step toward the East.

This book is a look at his thirty-two packed years and an analysis of the wave of martial arts films his name has become synonymous with.

Someday far down the line, after East and West have met, people will tell Bruce Lee stories in the same dreamy way people tell Jimmy Dean or Buddy Holly or Janis Joplin stories.

In this book I will attempt to portray Lee as I believe he would have wanted: in truth.

"In building a statue," Bruce Lee once told an interviewer, "a sculptor doesn't keep adding clay to his subject. Actually, he keeps chiseling away at the unessentials until the truth of his creation is revealed without obstructions."

For all time forward, martial artists and especially martial arts film stars will be compared to Bruce Lee by audiences and critics. This book is an attempt to explain the man who lives on in legend.

I would like to thank some very special people who made this book possible. There are many others I will not mention, but I want them to know they, too, have my thanks.

First off, my warmest regards to Linda (Mrs. Bruce) Lee, who gave freely of her time and energy in this project, although she neither authorized nor approved the final manuscript. A similar thanks to Bruce's mother, Mrs. Grace Li, and her sons, Robert and Peter. Deepest personal regards to Frank Price, Marvin Farkas, Michael Chugani, Norman Barrymaine, Eric Lacitis, Frank Chesley, Pete Liddell, and everyone at Shaw Brothers studio.

Many thanks to Gloria Safier, Liz Smith, Sherwood Salvan, Elaine Deckert, Terry Johnson King, Howard Kleinberg, Lee and Ted Crail, Henry Gellis, Janet Cubit, Ed Parker, Peter Urban, Ram Bam, Bob MacLaughlin, Buddha, Hermann Hesse, Uncle Dirty, Linda Weintraub, Sterling Silliphant, Larry Block, Andre Morgan, Raymond Chow, Leo Wilder, Fred Weintraub, Paul Heller, Taky Kimura, Donald Lewis, and Robert, Anne, Rita, Paula and Lindsay Block.

A special thanks to Peter and Jeannie Wolf.

1

The Protector of San Francisco

"A man's nature is determined at three."
——CHINESE PROVERB

There is a tribe in Malaysia which believes Bruce Lee is still alive and his reported death on July 20, 1973, is merely a publicity stunt for a film he was working on then, "The Game of Death."

They believe he will rise from the grave at some future time and prove once and for all he is bigger than life. Meanwhile, they continue to view his films waiting for his return.

When Bruce Lee died at the age of thirty-two with heart-shattering unpredictability, many who knew him or knew of him expressed disbelief; but those who have been dragged through autopsy, circus-like coroner's hearing, two funerals, insurance investigations and pages of false dirt in the sensationalist press know well he is no longer around to defend himself against lies or legend-makers.

What killed him? There are numerous theories. The Hong Kong coroner returned a verdict of "misadventure," which is a bit different from calling his death "accidental," but no one is sure exactly how he died.

The only sure thing is that a blood vessel burst in his brain while he was resting from a headache at the home of Taiwanese actress Betty Ting-pei, with whom he had been discussing a script for their upcoming film.

We will look fully at all the circumstances surround-

ing Bruce Lee's death later, but I think it is more
important first to recall him in life.

Bruce Lee loved life, his wife, fame, fortune, the
martial arts, and he had it all. He had a deep personal
philosophy and constant involvement with the challenge of survival. He had millions of idolizing fans and
could see his picture on the cover of dozens of fan
magazines all over the Orient, and if he looked hard
enough, all over the world.

His success had come after years of frustration as
an actor. Years in which he couldn't get major roles in
the West because the big studios and networks didn't
trust him to attract an audience; and the big studios in
the East wouldn't recognize he was different from
anyone else.

When Lee had gone to the Orient in 1970 on a
vacation trip, Asia's most important studio mogul,
Run Run Shaw of Shaw Brothers, had offered him a
typical Asian contract player's deal: a six-year contract for $75 a week.

"He was just another actor," recalls Run Run Shaw.
"Who knew?"

Less than three years later Shaw offered Lee an
estimated $250,000 for a single film, and Lee turned
it down, demanding an estimated $400,000. Shaw
accepted, but the film could never be made.

How did Bruce Lee reach such heights?

The story begins with a small Eurasian woman in
San Francisco's Chinese Hospital on November 27,
1940. Her name was Grace Li, and her husband was
three thousand miles away in New York's Chinatown
doing comedy on the stage of the Cantonese Opera,
a sort of Chinese vaudeville. Her family was five thousand miles in the other direction, in Hong Kong.

The child she bore that day was her second son in
thirteen months, and fourth child overall. He was born
in the year of the Dragon, during the morning hour of
the Dragon. She named him Lee Yuen Kam, using the
Americanized spelling of Li since he was born in

America. The name meant, literally, "Protector of San Francisco." "We were alone," recalls Grace Li, "and he was my protector."

The Chinese characters were changed slightly a few months later, says Grace Li, because the Chinese pictographs were the same as his late grandfather's. Although in the West the sameness in names would be an honor, the name had to be changed for Eastern superstitious reasons. His family usually called him "The Little Phoenix," a female name meant to confuse evil spirits who steal precious little boys after dark. To his fans, he became Lee Siu Loong, "The Little Dragon."

A nurse in the hospital decided the infant needed an even more American name and dubbed the baby boy Bruce Lee. It wasn't until thirteen years later, when he enrolled in an English school in Hong Kong, that he again heard his American name. It was the same year he began seriously studying the martial arts.

Bruce Lee was a precocious child. His older brother Peter, now a scientist with the Royal Observatory in Hong Kong, recalls whenever Bruce sat still people would think he must be sick. He was forever jumping, talking, playing or moving. Then just as suddenly he could disappear into his room or a far corner and read a book for hours or become completely self-absorbed.

Bruce played the first of his twenty childhood film roles when he was six years old, after being introduced to the movie industry through friends of his father's. He was always a low-paid supporting actor, except in one film when he was eighteen. He had been carried on as a human prop in a film when he was six months old, but dated his true screen debut to a crude film called "The Beginning of a Boy," when he was six.

In this forgettable flick Lee's screen dad is an honest, hard-working clerk, while his mother is a flighty woman who gambles away the family's savings at mah jong.

The six-year-old Lee is already getting his way on

screen, pushing his nose in where it doesn't belong. After a tiff with his mother, the little boy runs away to climb a far-off mountain which he has been told is magic. If he survives the Mountain of Tigers, he will return with the strength of ten men.

He eludes bandits and tigers, clicking away in crudely edited black and white, and arrives cold and hungry at a monastery half way to the summit. Monks feed him and put him to work chopping wood, running errands, whatever. He flees and returns to his home city where he joins a gang and becomes a pickpocket. One day he picks his father's pocket and is recognized. He takes off with his dad in hot pursuit, runs into the path of an oncoming car, and is hit. His father carries his limp form home for Bruce Lee's first death scene.

As Lee's celluloid presence falters, his father says he should have worked harder and his mother says she should have gambled less. She admits he ran away because she had lost her temper with him, mainly because she was in a bad mood over her gambling losses. The kid dies. Curtain.

Bruce Lee never acted with his real father, Lee Hoi Chuen, either on stage or screen. This comedian in the Cantonese Opera was given to much costuming and great dynamic flourish on stage. While he couldn't by any stretch of the imagination be called a famous personality on a grand scale, Lee Hoi Chuen was quite well known among patrons of his art form.

The Cantonese Opera was never held in the same kind of respect as the Peking Opera, which is what people usually mean when they say "Chinese Opera." The difference would be comparable to that between the Palace Theater of classic vaudeville days and the Metropolitan Opera.

Like vaudeville, the Cantonese Opera has pretty much disappeared, a victim of movies, television and modern times. The Peking Opera is still carried on.

Bruce Lee's second film role had him again as the abandoned child. By this time he was known on screen as Lee Siu Loong, or The Little Dragon. It is this name he was best known by in Hong Kong and on the Mandarin film circuit.

In his second film, made when he was about eight, Lee plays a doorstep baby, ignored by his wealthy father, abandoned by his serving-girl mother. He is taken in by a gambler and sold into servitude. He is again a tough little kid on camera and even gets to push a little girl around. In the end, with his role played by an adult, the Lee character has become a celebrated doctor. He operates on the sweetheart of his youth and restores her sight as he once promised. His real father and his foster father return to fawn over him, but he ignores them. Fade.

According to his brother Peter, Bruce actually thought about a career in medicine. When he was in early adolescence he would tell people his ambition was to be an M.D.

Things were pretty good at home for young Bruce, although his mother says she only let him make movies on school vacations. His family was affluent and large with many connections and friends. His father was originally from the village of Fat Shan in Canton. His mother was raised in Shanghai and brought to Hong Kong at nineteen where she met and married Lee Hoi Chuen.

During Bruce's formative years they lived near the peak on Hong Kong island with an aunt and uncle. Bruce's father helped raise a boy named Wu Ngan, who later served Bruce as a sort of all-purpose man Friday.

Even as a boy, Bruce was considered fairly good-looking and knew it. He liked to have his own way and by the time he was a teenager he was an out-and-out bully. He had a natural flair for leadership and liked to show off and lead the local neighborhood street gangs.

In one encounter Bruce got his head nearly knocked off and was inspired at thirteen to begin serious study of the martial arts as self-defense.

Lee Hoi Chuen had been a student of the martial arts and shared some of his knowledge with his son. Bruce always said his father was his first martial arts teacher. In Hong Kong it is common practice for the men, by the hundreds, to go out each morning in local parks to practice Tai Chi Chuan, and Bruce would go along with his father.

Tai Chi Chuan, called Tai Chi in the West, is a series of forms done in slow motion and particular sequence. Once mastered, it is exercise, mental health therapy and self-defense. Run Run Shaw, master of Shaw Brothers film studio, does at least a half hour every morning. It is perfect for businessmen, he says, because it can be done in an open field, an office or a hotel room on the road. It develops grace and teaches efficiency of movement.

Lee Hoi Chuen might well have told his son the mythical story of the origin of Tai Chi. It is attributed to a Chinese Taoist monk named Chang San-feng.

As the story goes, Chang San-feng was in his home meditating at noontime one day when he heard an unusual noise outside. Looking into the courtyard from his window he saw a snake, head raised tautly, hissing a challenge to a crane in the tree above. According to Da Liu in his *T'ai Chi Ch'uan and I Ching*, the crane flew down from the pine tree and attacked the snake with its swordlike beak. But the snake turned its head aside and attacked the crane's neck with its tail. The crane used its right wing to protect its neck. Then the snake darted against the crane's legs. The crane raised its left leg and lowered its left wing to combat the assailant. Stabbing again and again, the bird was unable to make a solid blow. The snake, twisting and bending, was always out of reach. After a while, tired of fighting, the crane flew back to the tree and the snake slithered into the hole in the tree trunk. There they rested in preparation for their encounter the following day.

". . . From (this incident) he realized the value of

yielding in the face of strength. In the combat of the crane and the snake, he saw in living form the principle of the *I Ching*: the strong changing to the yielding and the yielding changing to the strong. He remembered the teaching: 'What is more yielding than water? Yet back it comes to wear down the stone.' The great master studied the crane and the snake, the wild animals, the clouds, the water and the trees bending in the wind. He codified these natural movements into a system of exercise."

Later in life, when he became a teacher, Bruce Lee often used the example of flowing like water and yielding to the other man's strength until you wore him away.

Bruce began studying Chinese kung fu, or Chinese boxing, which he always pronounced "gung fu," when he was thirteen.

"As a kid in Hong Kong," Bruce recalled for *Black Belt Magazine* in October 1967, "I was a punk and went looking for fights. We used chains and pens with knives hidden inside. Then, one day, I wondered what would happen if I didn't have my gang behind me if I got into a fight. I decided to learn how to protect myself and I began to study gung fu."

Bruce enrolled in the Wing Cheun School and studied for the next two years with Yip Man. According to a later Golden Harvest documentary on Bruce, one trick he used to pull to get private instruction from his group's teacher was to stand on the stairs before class waving off his fellow pupils. "No class tonight," he would tell them. Then, very innocently, he would show up in class as the only student.

About the same time Bruce was enrolled by his family in St. Francis Xavier College. He was never much of a student because most of the time he found it difficult to sit still.

Bruce did manage to win the Inter-School Boxing Championship of Hong Kong and was an excellent dancer. He hardly ever lacked for dancing partners, either. According to his brother Peter, Bruce always had lots of dates. From the time he was fifteen, according to Peter, girls would regularly pursue him.

Peter, by the way, never seriously studied the martial arts, but was for a time fencing champion of Hong Kong.

Bruce, recalls Peter, who is thirteen months older, used to spend fifteen or twenty minutes in front of the mirror each morning greasing his hair just right and admiring himself. It was his morning ritual, just as important as making sure he was always sharply and nattily attired. Later in life he flaunted Eastern and Western convention and dressed "cool," like a suave hipster.

Once Bruce was committed to kung fu, he was nearly fanatic. He would sit at dinner pounding one hand on a stool at his side to toughen it even as he ate and made conversation. He had to be tough because he regularly shot his mouth off at anyone who he felt had slighted him. He felt he had to instantly avenge any slight, not just to his own honor, but to that of any member of his family.

Bruce, who was fourth-born of five children, got only smiles from his older sisters, Agnes, now a medical technician in Pennsylvania, and Phoebe, now married and working as a bookkeeper in San Francisco. Bruce's younger brother Robert lives with his mother in Los Angeles where he is a student.

Bruce and Peter were fairly close until they were about fifteen or sixteen, then began to drift apart. Bruce had a scar as a reminder of his brother from a time Peter let him have it mid-lip with a toy gun.

Bruce's toys as he got older were girls and more girls. He could charm, cajole, joke and dance for hours. He once had cards made up which he would hand to girls, with the Chinese equivalent on them of: "I'd like to make you. If the answer is yes, smile." Later, even after he was married, he'd open conversations with new single girls by asking if they would like to go to bed with him. If his wife was around, he might just invite them to punch his stomach of steel.

Bruce was a fantastic dancer and in 1958, shortly before he left Hong Kong, he won a Crown Colony cha-cha championship.

Since Bruce had been born in the U.S., he had to decide when he reached eighteen if he wanted to go to the States to retain his U.S. citizenship. He did and in the fall of 1958, with only $100 to his name, Bruce booked passage to San Francisco third-class on a freighter.

His film in which he had his first starring role had just finished its premiere run as Bruce left. It was called "The Orphan," and was about street gangs in Hong Kong a la "Blackboard Jungle."

In the film the two most important gangs are the 14 K's and the Wo Sing Wo (and a moll gang called the 18 Sisters). Bruce has been orphaned during the Japanese occupation but survives the flying lead, bombings, and hunger and becomes a street urchin whose specialty is, once again, picking pockets. A high-thinking man befriends him, but Lee spurns the offer of aid. Then he is arrested and given the choice of seven years' jail or school. He chooses school. Unfortunately, his friends talk him into one last caper. He agrees but later cops out at the last minute and his street pals cut his ears off.

That, of course, was fiction. William Cheong, who now runs a restaurant called the Dragon Inn in Canberra, Australia, recently recalled for a Hong Kong newspaper what he claims are facts.

Cheong says he was friends with Bruce and worked out with him daily for five years until he sailed for San Francisco in 1958. Cheong says he was known as The Big Dragon while Lee, of course, was known in Chinese as The Little Dragon. Cheong says they took on all comers in fights.

"We were very unpopular with rival gangs, especially Bruce," Cheong recalled for Robin Alp in Sydney, "because of our reputations as good fighters. Bruce was particularly unpopular because he was very cheeky and thought he could outfight anybody."

"It was a good time," recalls Peter Li, "for Bruce to leave Hong Kong when he sailed off to America. He had made quite a few enemies and some of them were talking about killing him."

2

Gung Ho for Kung Fu

"158.   Let a wise man first go the right way himself, then teach others. So he will have no cause to grieve."

"159.   The man who makes himself as he teaches others, being himself controlled, will be able to control others. The self is hard to control."

"160.   Who else but the self can be master of the self? With self well controlled, another master is hard to find."

"165.   By oneself evil is done; by oneself one suffers. By oneself evil is left undone; by oneself one is purified. Purity and impurity are personal concerns. No one can purify another."

"166.   Let no man neglect his duty for another's. Clearly seeing what is best for him, let a man attend to it."

—From the Dhammapada of Buddha,
quoted from *The Wisdom of Buddhism*

In "The Way of the Dragon," the only film Bruce Lee ever directed, he plays the part of a country boy who leaves his family in Hong Kong to go to Rome, where he is to protect his cousin's Chinese restaurant from takeover by a rather inept branch of organized crime.

Lee wrote the script as well as starring and portrays a bumpkin who is shy of girls but not a fight. He likes to eat and practice his kung fu.

Was that anything like the real Bruce Lee arriving after a long ship passage in San Francisco? Probably not. The real Bruce Lee already spoke English from his years of erratic study at a string of schools he was either expelled from or left for a variety of reasons. If anything, San Francisco was probably a letdown for the energetic eighteen-year-old.

In Hong Kong he was already a well-known movie actor. In the States he was just another Chink. He was so bothered by the image of the Chinese in the United States that he immediately gave up any hope of acting in his new home.

"When I went back to the States," Lee recalled, "I said, 'Here I am, a Chinese, not prejudiced or anything, just realistic thinking.' How many times in (Hollywood) films is a Chinese required? And when it is required, it is always branded as the typical tung, dung, tung, tung, tung, with the little pigtail in back . . . You know the type. So I said the hell with it."

It was this attitude that later endeared Bruce Lee to the people of Hong Kong. Perhaps the most famous line he ever spoke on film, from the Hong Kong audience's point of view, was in "The Chinese Connection" when he said, "The Chinese are not the sick men of Asia."

Bruce knew there were few parts for Orientals and most of what there was usually went to Japanese actors. He also knew, or learned quickly, there is tremendous prejudice in the Western world against the Chinese. Since the days they built the railroads for pennies an hour, since the days the Chinese were crushed in the Boxer Rebellion, and as part of the anti-Communist feeling after 1949, they have been generally looked down upon in the West.

Most Occidentals don't understand the Chinese and until recently most didn't care to make the effort. The Chinese in the States were a small, hard-working minority who didn't make much noise and liked to live among themselves in "Chinatowns."

What Bruce Lee found when he arrived in San Francisco was a caste system that either placed Chinese low on the totem pole or ignored them. The other prevalent attitude was a vestige of McCarthyism, still rampant in the late Fifties, that tended to mistrust anyone who didn't immediately swear allegiance to Chiang Kai-shek and labeled them "Commies." In the consciousness of many Americans during the Fifties and Sixties, China simply did not exist except as a goblin buddy of Russia.

Bruce Lee's more immediate problem upon his arrival was his living conditions. Through his family he was placed with a friend of his father's in San Francisco, a very old man, who had no control over the young man at all. For a short time Bruce gave dancing lessons to earn pocket money. The two never got along, however, and Bruce jumped at the chance a few months later to move to Seattle where he would live above a Chinese restaurant and work part-time as a waiter.

The restaurant is still there today, run by the same woman, Ruby Chow. It is a big old house, with additions and office buildings built up all around it now, on a hill almost directly across from Seattle University.

Ruby Chow, whose name is out front in red neon, is a well-known local spokeswoman for the Chinese community, active in politics. She is a woman of opinions and strong will. She and Bruce, whom she accepted because she knew his father, never got along too well and even now her memories are not pleasant.

At eighteen Bruce was outspoken and powerful. He was already teaching a few friends the way of kung fu and attended Edison Vocational High School days. Nights he would either work in the restaurant as a waiter or busboy or practice his kung fu. Sometimes he combined the two, setting up a pad in a back corner of the kitchen. Between customers, he would bounce up and down, practice his kata (form) and punch or jab at the cushion.

Bruce's problem in school was that they made him take subjects they thought would help him, like math and science, instead of those he preferred, like history and philosophy. He would do well in those he liked and badly in those he found distasteful.

He did manage to get a high school diploma from Edison and went on to enter the University of Washington as a philosophy major. He stayed there three years, but never graduated.

When he was nineteen, Bruce met a short, likable Japanese-American businessman named Takauki Kimura, then thirty-eight, who became his disciple and best friend. Taky Kimura had been robbed of his own youth by World War II.

The Kimuras had been the only Oriental family in their small West Coast town. In 1942 the authorities had come and demanded they be handed over for internment for the duration of the war in one of the American concentration camps for people of Japanese ancestry. Kimura recalls the town fathers had pleaded to leave the family be, pointing out they had never hurt anyone. The rule had been hard and fast and at eighteen Taky had been taken away.

Taky is now a successful grocer in Seattle and remembers the experience with some interesting perspective. He was in the camp until 1947 and says he emerged with his self-image destroyed. To add to his troubles, he couldn't find a job. When he would apply at a place with a "Help Wanted" sign in the window, they would look at his Oriental features and announce they had no openings.

Taky began rebuilding his self-confidence through judo. After he met Bruce and began to train intensively in Jeet Kune Do (although that name came later), he was finally able to get himself back together.

"Even then," Taky Kimura recalls, "Bruce was the leader. He had a special kind of presence. As soon as he would enter a room, everyone would turn in his direction."

Bruce began taking pupils and shortly founded the Jun Fan Gung Fu Institute (the name incorporates a form of his Chinese name, so that it is also known as the Bruce Lee School).

The school's first real home was in a basement in Seattle's Chinatown. Bruce didn't believe in advertising in the media or even hanging out a big sign. He followed the traditional method of attracting students, which was to let the school's reputation do the attracting. This appealed to Bruce's sense of dignity and tradition and his need to make himself the center of a cult. Although he often talked of opening a chain of kung fu schools, and had the opportunity offered by promoters, he never did so because he would have lost quality control and the feeling of a small group dedicated to an art and an artist. The artist, of course, had to be Bruce.

Bruce, Taky and some of the students did go around giving demonstrations for university students. Taky Kimura recalls they would often go to fraternity houses and Bruce would demonstrate his skills. There was a minimum of ritual and a maximum of showmanship.

Bruce Lee always believed specific styles and dogma should never get in the way of a martial artist fulfilling his potential. Bruce complained in his 1967 *Black Belt* interview that classical forms, rituals and "unreasonable stances" most students learn are worthless. "It's just too artificial and mechanical and doesn't really prepare a student for actual combat. A guy could get clobbered while getting into his classical mess. Classical methods like these, which I consider a form of paralysis, only solidify and condition what was once fluid. Their practitioners are merely blindly rehearsing systematic routines and stunts that will lead to nowhere.

"Bruce," adds *Black Belt*, "characterizes this type of teaching as nothing more than 'organized despair.'

"Basically, his technique is to proceed instantly and

unceremoniously to knock his adversary flat on his
wallet before he can even remember why he picked
on him in the first place."

After Bruce had moved from Edison High to the
university, he rented space in an office building near
the campus and expanded his school.

"Bruce was one person," recalls Taky, "who, if he
told you something, could do it too. He was outspoken.

"Like Bob Wall (West Coast karate teacher) said,
'The one thing I hate about Bruce is he can do anything he says.' A lot of people took exception, but
when they saw what he could do, they all wanted to
join him.

"You could show him something," adds Taky, "and
the next time you saw him he was doing it better
than you . . . He was one of the most powerful and
graceful people I have ever seen."

Taky recalls a time when Bruce was still a student
at Edison High and a Japanese karate sensei, fanati-
cally proud of his own system, took Bruce's comments
as a personal affront. He came to a demonstration
and challenged Bruce to a fight. Bruce declined. The
Japanese insisted and left Bruce with no choice except
to lose face, which he would never accept.

Bruce won in eleven seconds. The Japanese became a close friend of Bruce's, almost a follower.

One of Bruce's favorite pastimes was going with
Taky to the boxing matches. "He was like a coach
watching a football game," recalls Taky. "He'd constantly tell me a guy should do this, or a guy should
do that."

Taky says Bruce dated a lot, but not usually the
same girls for any length of time. He loved going to
the movies, especially the action films.

Bruce's one embarrassment was his English. Even
though it was quite good for someone who had been
in the States only a short time, he took a couple of
courses to improve it, at Edison and at the University
of Washington.

Another course at the university Bruce enjoyed was art. His former teacher there still has some of Bruce's paintings, bold men in action poses with an Oriental flair, hanging in her office.

Although his family could have afforded to send him money to help out, Bruce always prided himself that he never had to ask. He had grown to his full five-foot seven and one-half inches, one hundred forty pounds, and lived frugally but in as healthy a manner as possible. Besides regular training he did not smoke, rarely drank and used few drugs, even aspirin.

As Ruby Chow recalls, neither did he pay rent.

Bruce's consuming passion was the martial arts. It determined his friends. It brought him fame, fortune and even a wife. It was his way of muscling out a place in the world.

"It's really a simple plot," Bruce said, describing "Way of the Dragon," "of a country boy going to a place where he cannot speak the language, but somehow he comes out on top because he honestly and simply expresses himself by beating the hell out of 'em."

3

Lady Love a Dragon

"The five colors can blind,
The five tones deafen,
The five tastes cloy.
The race, the hunt, can drive men mad
And their booty leave them no peace.
Therefore a sensible man
Prefers the inner to the outer eye:
He has his yes, he has his no."

—Lao Tzu

The thin, attractive brunette coed might first have heard about Bruce Lee's kung fu school attending one of the demonstrations he gave at the University of Washington gym. She might have read in the local papers of Lee's art: "Gung fu, sometimes called Chinese pugilism, is more than 4000 years old. The art, based on the principles of Taoism and Buddhism, is considered the ancestor of the Japanese ju jitsu and karate."

Whatever brought her, this sweet thin all-American-looking girl became one of Bruce Lee's most interested students during his third and, as it turned out, final year at the University of Washington. Her name was Linda Emery and she wasn't flashy or loud or fast, simply sensitive, intelligent and brunette.

She became part of the group around Bruce. They would practice kung fu together, often when the weather was good on a broad green lawn near the academic buildings. Afterward, they would go off to dinner together and then to a film. Then one day

Bruce asked Linda to sneak off with just him, just the two of them, to have dinner. They were married in a small Seattle Protestant church a short time later.

As a bachelor, Bruce liked to have affairs with beautiful, flashy girls, says his brother Peter, but he married a quiet, sensitive girl who knew how to listen and would let him have his way. "He knew what real beauty was," adds Peter, "and he knew she would take care of the family."

"He loved Linda for her sincerity and devotion," says Taky Kimura. "She had the kind of depth he had."

Linda flowered with Bruce. She had lost her own father when she was only four years old, and welcomed his authoritative ways. Her inner beauty showed up as a warm glow. He liked her at his side, well dressed and attentive, and she was there. When his temper flared, she was there to help him regain his calm. When he grew quiet, she knew to leave him alone.

"Bruce was always the center of attention," says Linda Lee, now once again living in Seattle. "He was the teacher. He was always better—sort of a step higher—than anyone else. I think people were afraid to get real close to him because they didn't feel like equals with him.

"He made many acquaintances but few deep personal friends. He would do anything for a really good friend."

Linda's place next to Bruce on the highway toward elusive success wasn't always paved with happiness. Nor was the road direct. The Lees were to move eleven times during their nine-year marriage.

The first move was to Oakland where Bruce and Linda lived with a friend Bruce had made when he first came to San Francisco, another kung fu artist, James Lee (who also died suddenly, just a year before Bruce). Bruce left Taky Kimura to run the dojo (school) or as Bruce called it, "the kwoon," in Seattle.

Bruce had done fairly well, grade-wise, at the Uni-

versity of Washington, but formal education appealed
to him no more than classical karate. It seemed too
restricting.

Bruce spent snatches of his spare time for months
working on a thesis about the martial arts, but finally
abandoned it because he felt it would be misused.
Meaning he felt someone else would try to systemize
his knowledge, which is exactly the opposite of the
message he was trying to spread.

"Many people who came to instruction," Bruce
said, "would say, like, 'Hey man, like what is the
truth? Hand it over to me.' So therefore one guy
would say, 'I'll give you my Japanese way of doing it.'
In Jeet Kune Do . . . nationalities don't mean anything. I mean, at least you can say there are different
approaches. We must approach it as an expression of
ourself. When you go to a Japanese style, then you are
expressing a Japanese style. You are not expressing
yourself."

It was this attitude that continuously upset the
established masters of the martial arts worldwide,
wherever Bruce went, since they spend their entire
lives seeing the universe as a single system.

Bruce even spurned colored belts and eventually
would take only students who had prior training, making Jeet Kune Do a kind of specialty graduate work
for all martial artists. In essence, Bruce tried to teach
applications of forms adapted to individual need,
while others taught the traditional way, by repetition.

"I don't have any belt whatsoever," said Bruce Lee.
"That is just a certificate. Unless you can really do it,
that belt doesn't mean anything. I think it might be
useful to hold your pants up, but that is about it."

Bruce and James Lee opened a Jun Fan School in
Oakland, which Bruce always referred to simply as
the "James Lee School."

To help promote the school, Bruce gave demonstrations at tournaments in various parts of the western
United States. One of the most important was the

Long Beach Tournament where Bruce gave a demonstration in 1964.

He had been invited by the tournament promoter, Ed Parker, a well-known Los Angeles instructor of Chinese karate. A six-foot, two-hundred-ten-pound Mormon who first learned his art in his native Honolulu, Parker is credited with introducing karate to a number of police departments; and has numbered among his students such Hollywood personalities as Frank Sinatra, Warren Beatty, Robert Wagner, Darren McGavin, MacDonald Carey, Rick Jason, Nick Adams and Blake Edwards.

Parker says in 1964 kung fu was still a relatively secret art. After meeting Bruce Lee through James Lee, whom Parker recalls as a great powerful hulk of a fellow, he invited him to give a demonstration at his tournament.

The reason kung fu, unlike karate or judo, was kept somewhat secret stems back to the Boxer Rebellion in China just after the turn of the century.

After increasing foreign exploitation from 1870 on, many Chinese began forming secret martial arts societies to rid themselves of the "foreign devils." By about 1900 the art of kung fu had reached a high level of perfection and an acceptance approaching religious frenzy.

Instructors recruited pupils by telling them a true master of kung fu could even laugh off the foreigners' guns and bombs.

Of course, history tells us they were wrong. The cream of the kung fu artists fought valiantly but lost to Western bullets. The forty-year foreign rape of China followed, until Mao Tse-tung took over in 1949.

After the rebellion a general rule that kung fu should be taught only to thoroughbred Chinese became an unwritten, sworn law. Bruce Lee was among the first to laugh off this law and make his art public. He told Parker he would be delighted to give an exhibition.

Interestingly, Parker considers the current craze for kung fu (which he correctly sees as a separate art from karate, aikido, hapkido or judo) comparable to the foolish talk spread in China just before the rebellion.

"Sure," says Parker, "it's like when the Boxer Rebellion came and the kung fu masters would tell the people not to worry about guns, to study harder at the fighting arts. Then they'd shoot blank guns off to show them no harm could come. Then guys would go out to fight thinking bullets couldn't hurt them and, of course, they got killed."

Parker says he found Bruce Lee brash at first, but was impressed by his talent. He pays Lee one of the highest compliments an instructor pays another martial artist. "He could make the air pop when he hit."

"Bruce was a cocky lad," adds Parker, echoing Taky Kimura, "but once you got to know him, he had a right to be.

"When he first came here, he knew only the Wing Cheun style, but he learned quickly."

Parker filmed Bruce's demonstration at the Long Beach Tournament.

Present at the tournament, and awed by Bruce's ability, was Jay Sebring, then one of the most fashionable hair stylists in Hollywood. Sebring later was murdered with Sharon Tate in a house in the Hollywood Hills by the Manson gang.

In 1964, after the tourney, Sebring had a chat with Lee. Not long afterward, Sebring was cutting William Dozier's hair when the TV producer mentioned that he was looking for someone to cast as Charlie Chan's Number One Son in a new series he planned. Dozier was then just hitting it big with "Batman," which became an instant smash as a mid-season replacement.

Sebring mentioned Lee and said he would probably be perfect.

Dozier was put in touch with Ed Parker who brought his film of Lee's exhibition over to Twentieth Century-Fox for a screening. Parker recalls Dozier was delighted.

Bruce was signed to an option.

Meanwhile, Bruce's Jun Fan School was not doing well in Oakland. Bruce screened pupils carefully, throwing out any who didn't appeal to him or who didn't seem serious enough. He was a perfectionist and tried to teach every class himself.

"He wasn't just teaching a set of rules to follow," says Linda Lee. "He was teaching a way to think of fighting. The way of the intercepting fist.

"With Bruce, they had to understand why they were making moves; and that there isn't just one answer for all situations. You have to be flexible. Bruce taught philosophy through the physical."

Bruce left Oakland to pursue Dozier's offer. He went with Linda to Los Angeles where he received his only formal acting instruction, one month at the Twentieth Century-Fox acting school.

While they settled in, Bruce started a third Jun Fan School in Los Angeles, and Linda gave birth to their first child.

In the same week in February 1965 that Brandon Bruce Lee was born, Lee Hoi Chuen, Bruce's father, died in Hong Kong.

Lee Hoi Chuen never wanted Bruce to be an actor. As with many actors, his chosen profession was not what he would have chosen for his son. Yet Bruce told Linda he felt a special closeness to his father, and had fond memories of going along for the experience when his father went on tour.

According to Grace Li, Lee Hoi Chuen had predicted when he was thirty-four, in 1935, that he would die when he was sixty-four years old. His prediction was fulfilled.

Bruce used the option money from Dozier to take Linda and Brandon to Hong Kong for the summer of 1965. Linda was readily accepted by the family but recalls she was not happy. "It was too hot," she says of the intolerably humid South Asian summer. "And there was nowhere to go to get away from it."

Brandon was less than six months old and suffered all the ills of infancy, from heat rash to colic. They lived in a small family apartment, crowded with relatives, friends coming and going, and Linda did not yet speak Cantonese. Few of Bruce's smiling relatives spoke any English either.

They returned to Seattle during the fall, still waiting for word from Dozier. The only messages were of more delays.

After a short post-New Year stay in Oakland, the three finally moved into a tiny apartment on Wilshire Boulevard in Los Angeles in March 1966.

Bruce by then knew the Number One Son idea was off, and had been set for "Green Hornet." Dozier told him the network was insisting "Batman" run for a full season first, before "The Green Hornet" could begin. The Green Hornet and Kato (played by Lee) did several guest appearances in preparation, but otherwise Lee did little acting.

To pass the time, Bruce opened his third kwoon, a tiny dojo in Los Angeles' Chinatown, with another old friend, Dan Inosantos.

At first Inosantos was just Lee's pupil. Soon he was running the kwoon when Bruce had to be away. They became fast friends.

"No other instructor could teach like him," recalls Inosantos, now a well-known sensei in Los Angeles. "He could be joking one minute, be serious another.

"He was of a caliber far beyond other martial artists. He's the Edison, Einstein and Leonardo da Vinci of the martial arts. Bruce reminded us of Jonathan Livingston Seagull because he was always striving to be better and better. If he had any shortcomings, he was such a perfectionist he couldn't stand anything that didn't come up to his standards."

Bruce and Dan Inosantos spent hours together, he recalls, just walking. Bruce loved to explore old bookstores and had a huge collection of books, not just on the martial arts, but on other fighting arts, from swords to American boxing and wrestling. He wanted to take it all and synthesize the best martial arts philosophy.

Linda says Bruce usually carried a book with him, even when he knew he probably would not have time to read it. Sometimes he would stand exercising, stretching, flexing and at the same time reading, intensely concentrating. Linda says she was always amazed that in the midst of kids crying, doors slamming, people coming and going, Bruce could continue to flex and read as if he were all alone in his own monk's cell.

Inosantos often accompanied Lee to tourneys and either performed with him or aided him. He says a typical demonstration would include some agility demonstrations, with things like finger jabbing and flashing kicks to show his incredible leg speed. He would do two-finger pushups or all-thumbs pushups. He would demonstrate various moves with lightning speed, throwing a punch but never striking, always stopping a whisker away. He would do "sticky hands," one of his favorite exercises, where he would touch wrists with another man and dare him to try to slap his hands away. Bruce was always quicker.

For show, Bruce would break boards. With one kick, on a good day, he could snap eight two-inch boards held together by masking tape. He did fail occasionally but always kept up until he succeeded.

Bruce could consistently snap, with a single kick, four or five two-inch boards.

One of the toughest stunts, and one most martial arts experts don't even like to attempt publicly, is kicking through boards that are dangled in the air without rigid support. In 1965 Bruce would regularly cut through two two-inch boards dangled before him.

Dan Inosantos says Bruce never really liked teaching very much, especially classes. He finally began teaching only by private lesson, often for $100 an hour up to $250 per hour, because he felt the best way to teach was one-on-one.

As Bruce would explain, *jeet* means to stalk or to intercept, *kune* means fist or style, and *do* means the way or the ultimate reality. It was a way of saying the real purpose of martial arts is not form. The ultimate is to reach your opponent and strike. The most obvious difference from classical form is the lack of the passive block, meaning Jeet Kune Do is mostly offensive moves.

Bruce explained that what he meant by being non-classical was not lack of form, but emphasis on efficiency of form. He defined efficiency, the first part of Jeet Kune Do, as a punch that reached its mark.

The second part, directness, Bruce liked best to illustrate. One day his brother Robert Li found him practicing with his nunchaku, the two sticks connected by a chain. As soon as Robert entered, Bruce flailed the nunchaku at his head. Robert ducked. The nunchaku turned out to be made of hard foam rubber. That was directness. For Robert it meant doing what comes most naturally, ducking.

There is a famous story about a Zen sword master named Bokuden in Japan who when he was very old accepted pupils for teaching. He had a great reputation and a young man came to him and asked to be his pupil. As was the practice of Zen masters, he decided to test the young man's patience. The master assigned the youth to the kitchen where for the following year he did only minor household duties. The young man grew more and more impatient. Finally, he went to Bokuden and asked when he was to begin instruction in the art of swordsmanship. He told Bokuden he thought the master was too old to teach and was simply using him to get free kitchen labor. Bokuden told him henceforth his instruction would start. The very next morning, while the youth was in the kitchen cleaning some vegetables, Bokuden suddenly appeared and began whacking at him with the broad side of a sword. From then on, the two never spoke. But without any notice, Bokuden would appear, any place or time, and begin whacking the youth. After a while, racked with painful welts, the young man got so he knew when the old man was even in the next room. He grew eyes in the back of his head. When the old man could no longer sneak up on the young man, the master broke his silence and began the actual instruction. The young man had learned the meaning of directness. He had learned to sense his opponent's very presence.

This was what Bruce Lee meant by directness, and it was a talent he himself had. He was in touch with the inner forces, what the Chinese call Chi, and was open and empty enough to receive and interpret the slightest vibration.

The third part of Jeet Kune Do was simplicity. "The best illustration," Bruce told *Black Belt* in 1967, "is something I borrowed from Ch'an (the Chinese name of Zen). Before I studied the art, a punch to me was just like a punch, a kick just like a kick. After I [only just] learned the art, a punch (was) no longer a punch, a kick no longer a kick. Now that I've (truly) understood the art, a punch is just like a punch, a kick just like a kick.

"The height of cultivation is really nothing special. It is merely simplicity, the ability to express the utmost with the minimum. It is the half-way cultivation that leads to ornamentation.

"(Jeet Kune Do) is basically a sophisticated fighting style stripped to its essentials. The disciples are very proud to be accepted in this exclusive style."

Keeping quality control on his schools, forming them into his personal cult, was always important to Bruce. His kwoon in Los Angeles' Chinatown was almost impossible to find without detailed instructions; and the only sign was a tombstone-shaped one near the door: "In memory of a once fluid man, crammed and distorted by the classical mess."

When teaching, Bruce was never solemn like many instructors. He would joke, tell a story and then somehow relate it all to the point he was trying to make. He had natural charm when he chose and was an excellent storyteller.

"He liked to talk in the future tense," says Inosantos. "He made predictions. He said the great boom in martial arts would come from Japan and get commercialized. He said Thai kick boxing would become very popular. He predicted karate will go away and, because of tournaments, eventually there will be only one universal style.

"You must realize the cause of your own ignorance, he would say. It teaches you to work with your shortcomings and work on your abilities."

"Ninety percent of Oriental self-defense is baloney," Lee once told John Owen of the *Seattle Post-Intelligencer*. "I teach the Jun Fan method . . . It isn't ritual and it isn't sport. It's self-defense."

It was also about this time Bruce told Linda he would never open a string of martial arts schools because it would only prostitute him. A contributing factor to that decision was his participation in "The Green Hornet."

"He was a martial artist," says Linda, "but an actor by profession."

4

Kato

"Chop-Socky Brings in Gold, But Treated Like 'Garbage.'"

—Headline in *Variety*,
October 1973

"You know why I got the 'Green Hornet' job," Bruce Lee once asked an interviewer in Hong Kong rhetorically, "because the hero's name was Brit Reed and I was the only Chinese guy in all of California who could pronounce Brit Reed, that's why."

Van Williams had the role of Brit Reed (the Green Hornet), based on the old radio series character, who was a crusading, crime-busting newspaperman for the *Daily Sentinel*, and Bruce Lee, of course, was Kato. They were a grim two-man vigilante committee who did in villains even more quickly than Batman and Robin. After all, Batman and Robin always took two half-hour episodes to catch their crooks, while the Green Hornet and Kato had only one episode.

They made thirty half-hour shows for the 1966–1967 TV season and were never a particularly big smash in the United States. Lee later said he thought the reason for their failure was that the show took a serious attitude where it should have been looser and more satirical.

Lee would not permit his art, gung fu, to be put in a bad light on the series. He refused to pretend he needed long drawn-out fights when a few swift blows would do. Instead he had the cameramen use slow motion, much like the "Kung Fu" television series did eight years later.

Lee did go along with lots of flash and showmanship. While he wouldn't use flying jumps in life, he did use them for effect on the series.

It was for his role as Kato that Lee first took up the nunchaku, or noon-chucks, with which he is now closely identified by Western audiences.

The nunchaku is made of two round or hexagonal rods of hardwood or pipe, connected by a length of chain, cord or leather, and is used as a flail or bludgeon or to strangle an opponent. Nunchakus are banned in many parts of the world, and possesison of a pair is a felony in California and Illinois.

"The nunchaku is a versatile device," *Newsweek* reported. "When the connecting cord is wrapped around a victim's neck, the two sticks give even a weak assailant enough leverage to throttle his foe. When one stick is held in the hand, the other can be swung with fearsome speed and power."

"Those sticks can generate 1600 pounds of pressure at the point of impact," says Joseph Artesi, director of a karate school in Bridgeton, New Jersey. "The human bone breaks at about 8½ pounds, so you get a tremendous overkill."

"That, of course, poses a problem for police," continues *Newsweek*. "In Baltimore, officers have been attacked several times with nunchakus, and in Detroit recently a youth was arrested for merely possessing a homemade pair."

"A warning should go out to karate schools, kids and parents that the sticks are against the law," says New York City policeman Albert Gotay, a police academy self-defense instructor who has seen more and more of these things being carried by street gangs.

What's odd about Bruce's close identity with the sticks is that he disapproved of weapons, believing the human body was the ultimate weapon. He used the nunchaku only because it was showy and looked flashy on camera. It was a prop.

When I was in Hong Kong recently, I saw cases of plastic toy nunchakus, in blister-packs with Bruce's color likeness, ready to be distributed to children by Golden Harvest, Bruce's old studio, as a publicity stunt. A promotion in dubious taste.

Bruce Lee's life was changed in many ways by his role in "The Green Hornet," and a chain reaction was set off that would eventually lead to his fame and to his death.

Suddenly, he was in demand for public appearances and his asking price quickly rose to several thousand dollars for an afternoon's visit. He rode on floats and appeared at openings, often in Kato's dark suit, chauffeur's cap and black mask.

His role as Kato also ended most of his group teaching duties. He gave only private instruction and numbered many of Hollywood's leading personalities among his pupils. The list included Lee Marvin, James Coburn, Steve McQueen, James Garner, producer Sterling Silliphant, producer Sy ("Tarzan") Weintraub, and basketball star Kareem Abdul Jabbar (Lew Alcindor).

Through his pupils Bruce got a number of television guest appearances as well. During the lean, frustrating years that followed, those guest appearances often paid the rent. Bruce was seen on series such as "Here Comes the Brides," "Blondie," and "Ironsides," and later did four episodes of "Longstreet."

He was also the technical advisor on several films and worked at various times with stars like Dean Martin and the late Sharon Tate.

His first American feature film role was MGM's "Marlowe," which starred James Garner.

There was always plenty of time for other diversions. Bruce could be the life of the party and was warmly welcomed in many Hollywood homes.

One of Bruce's favorite stunts with newspaper interviewers or at parties was the coin trick. Here is how it was described by John Owen of the *Seattle Post-Intelligencer* when Lee returned as a conquering hero

the Christmas after he finished "The Green Hornet":
" 'I'm going to try to pick that dime out of your palm. Don't let me do it,' Lee cautioned.

"His fingers poised above the upturned palm, then suddenly he grabbed. He was too slow. The sportswriter's fist closed with the speed of a steel trap.

" 'Hey,' Lee marveled, 'you've got pretty fast reflexes.'

"The reporter blushed becomingly.

" 'Let me see the dime,' Lee asked.

"The reporter opened his fist. In his palm was a penny. Lee was holding the dime.

"Boy I'm telling you Green Hornet. Just be glad he's on your side!"

Sterling Silliphant, Oscar-winning writer-producer ("The Poseidon Adventure"), says he once related a dream he had to Bruce Lee, who was giving him private instruction in Jeet Kune Do.

In the dream Silliphant has a flat tire out on a lonely highway. A car stops and four men walk menacingly toward him. Silliphant runs to a nearby wall, figuring it will eliminate his blind side, and stands ready for an attack.

"I asked Bruce what I should have done," he recalls. "He told me my first mistake was running to the wall where they then had me cornered. He said if I was sure they wanted to fight, and couldn't or wouldn't run, I should have charged them and taken the offensive . . . He said to immediately use finger jabs to take one guy's eyes out, then a solid kick to the knee to stun and disable one more. Then keep flanking those who remain. He said to use my longest weapon, my legs. Keep kicking knees. The kneecap breaks at seventy pounds pressure, a child's power."

Bruce's advice to women faced with a brute was even more direct. "I advise any female learning gung fu," he hold *Black Belt* in 1967, "that if they are ever attacked to hit 'em in the groin, poke 'em on the shins or the knees . . . and run like hell."

The point of all this being not only that Bruce was

against styles, he was intolerant of anyone who was involved in life for anything less than all-out victory.

From the time "The Green Hornet" ended until he went to Hong Kong and became a sensation five years later, Bruce Lee trained, taught, read, dreamed and, above all, choked with frustration.

He told people close to him, with fiery conviction, that he would be the biggest, most important film star in the world someday, and he really meant it.

He lived with Linda, Brandon, and later Shannon, in Los Angeles and survived on some television and film parts his students, like Silliphant, helped him arrange.

"My son is probably the only blond-haired, blue-eyed Chinaman in these parts," he told *Black Belt.*

It was never important to Bruce that he make friends, just followers. "Above all he had a way about him. When he ridiculed people, he wasn't very tactful," recalls sensei Ed Parker. "He didn't pull his punches at all. You don't make friends by telling people their way of doing things is full of shit.

"In Chinatown I'd hear how unhappy they were about Bruce. They'd call him a wise punk."

When Bruce knocked systems, he was going against all the teachings many other instructors have staked their lives and livelihoods on. Bruce simply wouldn't go along with a system that he felt held him back, nor would he accept the fact that systems might be necessary for others.

"The most common method of judging in karate tournaments is the point count system," writes Peter Urban in *The Karate Dojo*, in which the number of skillful strikes to vulnerable areas of the opponent are decided on by a group of experienced karate men coordinated by a chief referee. "Although this system has proved itself to be the best practical method of determining winners in contests, many karate men dislike it. They claim that it is an unfair method because a fighter who is strong and courageous will often take a blow in order to deliver his own: he is therefore not at his best within the rules of the orthodox point system."

Bruce always insisted on being at his best. "He was one in two billion," says Ed Parker. "If God could give a man all the natural talents, he had it. He was limited by his own philosophy, though. He used to use an analogy about a sculptor, how he has to chip away the unessentials to find the essential truth. If a guy doesn't have the natural talent Bruce had, he can chip all day and he isn't going to find what Bruce had.

"His problem as a teacher was that he could pass on his ideas, but not his talent, and you needed both for his philosophy to work."

Sterling Silliphant was a pupil of Bruce's, under the ideal conditions of private lessons, for two years, which he says is the longest anyone studied continuously with sensei Lee. They would meet at Silliphant's Beverly Hills home or at Bruce's home near Culver City in Los Angeles. Silliphant says Bruce could be a patient teacher as long as the pupil had the right desire. During the first year Silliphant shared his $100-an-hour lessons with Hollywood columnist Joe Hyams, who now studies with Ed Parker.

Silliphant was a successful producer and forty-nine years old when he began lessons. "You'd think Bruce would have wanted me as a pupil," says Silliphant, "after all he was an actor and I hire lots of actors . . . Instead it took me six months to find him, then Bruce said, 'Forget it. You've never had martial arts. You're too old to start.' He wasn't against old age, just against starting out old. I told him he didn't know anything about me. At USC I had the fastest reflexes of anyone ever tested. I have incredible eyesight. Tests show I have a highly competitive attitude. I'm a winner. I was three years varsity fencing at USC and we won the Pacific Coast championship. I'd kept up my fencing. 'All you have to do is teach me to apply my attitude,' I told Lee. 'Instead of a sword hitting, it'll be my body hitting.'"

Silliphant became Lee's pupil. He recalls Bruce's home was filled with training devices. He had a stretching device where you put your legs in loops and a pulley stretched you beyond human endurance. "No wonder they talked about Chinese torture," Sterling joked to Bruce.

One whole wall was lined with things to hit to toughen hands and feet. Lee used rice, sand, BBs and even green peas.

There were special bags for punching and kicking. There was one giant bag in the garage Silliphant says was five feet wide by eight feet high, and enveloped half the area. "It was mushy to absorb power and to force extra effort and extra force out of you if you were to have any impact. It was like kicking into a marshmallow bigger than you." Bruce could send it flying with his best kick.

There were devices that kicked back when you hit them, forcing you to duck or get clobbered.

One that Bruce designed, and a friend of James Lee's built, was an inclined frame with a giant spring extending out beneath it. At the end of the spring was a cushion. Bruce could set the degree of tension to simulate an attack being returned. It was only three or four feet high reflecting Bruce's belief low-line attacks were most effective.

"Bruce said the greatest thing in the world to kick was a tree," recalls Silliphant, now working with Irwin Allen at Twentieth Century-Fox. "Not a sapling either, a large palm tree. He said when you can kick so you aren't jarred, but the tree is jarred, then you will begin to understand a kick."

Bruce's favorite device was an umpire's pad, or air shield, for absorbing blows. He would hold it while someone threw his best punch, then the other would hold it while Bruce punched. Bruce was never shaken, but his pupil often ended up across the room stunned. He was as quick and powerful a puncher as he claimed to be.

Bruce had all the necessary head and body gear for

sparring, and that was a main part of the instruction.

Silliphant says Bruce once brought a young man, fresh from Hong Kong, to his house. The young man was supposed to be a "sticky hands" (quick wrist slap fighting) champion. "He put us in the ring together, and I beat him, badly, which made Bruce glow with pride. The boy stormed out, angered with embarrassment, and would never talk to Bruce again. He just wasn't prepared for my improvisation, which Bruce taught, and he was unable to adjust to my ego, although I could adjust to his ego. 'You ignored his formality,' Bruce told me, 'and just went in and hit him.'

"He taught us only to win, not to lose. He called katas (forms done in practice like ballet exercise) 'vertical death.'"

Bruce also had an extensive collection of ancient and modern weapons. He had clubs, knives, fake guns, flailing devices, numerous swords of all types, and unusual ancient Chinese weapons.

As he went along, his instruction was increasingly influenced by American boxing, which he freely improvised into Jeet Kune Do.

"In my whole life," says Silliphant, "no man, no woman was ever as exciting as Bruce Lee because of his improvisational ability."

Silliphant introduced Bruce to actor James Coburn, who became a student and friend as well. Both also helped Bruce get parts in TV shows and films whenever they could.

"Jimmy Coburn and I became, really, in a sense, his personal advisors," says Silliphant. "Even saying how much he should get for a job, a shot on a TV series, for instance."

All his teaching was geared toward real fighting. One point he stressed was understanding "the gap," the space between you and your opponent. He said to relate to your opponent and learn his weaknesses.

"Bruce studied all techniques," says Linda Lee, "not only to know a system but to know what he was up against and to synthesize new movements from it. He would analyze the source of force, find its truth and efficiency of movement. He'd work on things instead of accepting things. He loved fencing for small moves and could adapt foil moves to his own needs, just as he adapted wrestling techniques."

The difference between other systems of martial arts and Bruce's was the difference between the pre-1800 British way of standing in formation to fight and Vietnam era guerrilla warfare. He would do anything necessary to win.

"He made you—without realizing it—get to the essence of what combat is," says Silliphant, "which is to deliver a blow to your opponent."

Coburn, Silliphant and Lee decided they wanted to do a film together, the "definitive film on martial arts." So in 1969 they hired a writer, with Silliphant and Coburn putting up a $12,000 fee, to write a script. They developed a story and told the writer to do it.

"He brought in a script," recalls Silliphant, "that was mostly science fiction and screwing. None of our plot. So we fired him."

Next, Mark Silliphant, Sterling's nephew who is also a writer, tried, and again the three were unhappy with the result.

Finally they agreed they would have to do it themselves. They decided to meet from four to six p.m., every Monday, Wednesday and Friday, without fail or excuses, above work and family, until it was done. Over the next year they laid out the film shot by shot, always ending at six o'clock on the dot.

Next Silliphant wrote the script in his spare time over three months and sent "The Silent Flute" off to a producer at Warner Brothers.

After negotiation the studio agreed, but with a big IF, if they would make the film in India, where the studio had "blocked rupees" (money earned in India but which they could not take out of the country), then Warner's would go along with the project.

None of the three was happy with India as a locale

for scenes placed in China, but they agreed to scout locations.

Coburn was to be the star of the film, at least on the marquee, but Bruce Lee was to play five roles and almost dominate the story.

Coburn, Silliphant and Lee spent three difficult weeks together in Pakistan and India scouting locations. They visited camel country in the North, walked the beautiful beaches of Goa, viewed the masses in poverty in Madras, Bombay and a lot of smaller places in between.

Bruce, says Silliphant, loved to amuse kids and constantly did sleight-of-hand tricks or kicks or punches. Although Western tourists are a common sight in India, a Chinese stood out. Few are seen.

"Bruce was always staging little shows," recalls Silliphant. "He could make coins disappear, or even a fork or knife seem to vanish."

A subtle friction developed. Coburn liked to keep a low profile while traveling, and Lee's stunts kept gathering crowds.

Bruce felt anger toward Coburn for things beyond their control. At hotels like the Taj Mahal in Bombay, Coburn, "the star," would be given an elegant suite while Lee and Silliphant would simply get nice rooms.

"Bruce came to me one evening," Silliphant recalls, "and said, 'I'm the star, not him.' For the first time I realized my guru wasn't just a great martial artist; he was also an actor filled with ego. I didn't respect him any less; I saw him more realistically.

"He said then he'd be the biggest star in the world, bigger than Coburn or McQueen.

"I said, 'No way. You're a Chinese in a white man's world.'

"Then he went out and did it."

By the time they returned home, the only thing they could agree on was that they did not want to do "The Silent Flute" in India. Coburn absolutely refused to do it in India, out of artistic conviction, says Silliphant.

"I thought we should do it just to get a jump on the market," Silliphant adds. "Bruce wanted the picture made for emotional reasons, at all costs."

Coburn's refusal caused Warner Brothers to drop out.

Shortly after, Bruce left for Hong Kong to make "Fists of Fury."

"The minute Bruce left me I got out of the aura a master gives," says Silliphant, who now studies Japanese karate. "I was nothing. And when I tried to apply what Bruce had taught me (in Japanese-style karate) against Black Belts, I couldn't use it because I didn't have the youth, power and speed of Bruce Lee. I had to start at the bottom and learn all over again."

"People ask me as an actor, 'How good are you really in gung fu?'" Lee told *Black Belt* in 1967. "I always kid them about that. If I tell them I'm good, they'll probably say I'm boasting, but if I tell them I'm no good, I'm lying. I tell them to believe half of what they see and nothing that they hear—and remember, seven hundred million Chinese can't be Wong."

5

The Feast in Hollywood East

"People around the world are enjoying Chinese food—
I don't see why they shouldn't take to Chinese films."

—Run Run Shaw

"The tongue is soft and remains, the teeth are hard and
fall out."

—Chinese proverb

Ten-year-old Tatum O'Neal, star of "Paper Moon,"
was asked to name her favorite movie. Without hesita-
tion she said "Five Fingers of Death."

A slight, wiry Chinese of sixty-plus years smiles
slightly when he hears about Tatum's tastes, but
admits he has never heard of Tatum O'Neal. He has
heard of "Five Fingers of Death." It was created by
his studio, Shaw Brothers of Hong Kong, as are two-
thirds of all the Chinese films produced in the world.

His name is Run Run Shaw and he and his brothers are an Asian legend. I'm going to take you on a
trip to meet him and to try to explain the Hong Kong
film industry, one of the five most productive celluloid
dream industries in creation.

Bruce Lee had a huge impact on Hong Kong's film-
makers, an impact some believe might even have
marked him for death. And considering what Lee was
up against, this impact is truly remarkable.

The average Chinese film (by which I mean the
product of the Hong Kong industry; the People's
Republic of China does make specialized "tractor"
films and revolutionary films which don't get distribu-

tion in the West) costs around $100,000 to make, although the figure has been rising steadily in the past few years. That is still about a tenth of the cost of an average Hollywood feature. Most films in Hong Kong are shot without sound, although actors move their mouths on cue, after which they are dubbed into whatever language is desired, usually Mandarin Chinese, just as the Italians have been doing with their spaghetti westerns for years.

Scripts are often simply copies of a Western-world film (Run Run Shaw will deny this, but more about him later) or are improvised as the crew goes along.

Scriptwriters who sell the studios original ideas get about $1800 for a script. Top directors get around $1800 for a film, and the biggest stars, until Bruce Lee came along, got (and most still get) less than $3000 per film.

Angela Mao-ying, who makes films for Raymond Chow's Golden Harvest (as did Bruce Lee), made ten films in three years, all of which were financially successful. Her face is known all over the globe and her film "Lady Whirlwind," released in America as "Deep Thrust," grossed $4 million in the U.S. alone. Her "Lady Kung Fu" was expected to gross more than a million dollars in the U.S.

How well is Angela paid? She gets a flat $150 per week and isn't allowed script approval or choice of directors. She lives in a four-room flat in the company dormitory and has no say over costars, locations or themes. She has a vague suspicion she is being exploited, but no idea how well her films have done around the globe.

The contemporary Hong Kong industry dates back to about 1949 when Chinese film-makers migrated from Shanghai just before the Communist takeover. Prosperity, which has now arrived in buckets of gold, is even newer. But the way it stands, with the right distribution almost any action or semi-sex film can make money.

Robert S. Elegant of the *Los Angeles Times*

described where the plots come from. "The Cantonese call it 'warming over yesterday's cold rice,' the scriptwriter explained. The normal approach in the beginning was for director, producer and writer to get together and say: 'You remember such and such? Well, we'll do it again this way.' First, it was the dramas of the 1930s they copied, then knight-errant and Imperial Court movies in gorgeous costumes. Later, Japanese films became the model and, shortly thereafter, the movies made by the Communists on the mainland."

At that time Nationalist Chinese Generalissimo Chiang Kai-shek in exile on Taiwan would ask regularly, "Is there anything new from Hong Kong?" Taiwan couldn't import mainland films, even though the patriotic themes were highly attractive to the Nationalists.

Elegant reports, " 'When in 1966 the Cultural Revolution ended the phase of semi-bourgeois movies in China,' the scriptwriter continued, 'Hong Kong began imitating American and European films. We call them chwan-tow (fist) and jung-tow (pillow) movies—violence and sex.' "

According to National General, which distributed "Chinese Connection" and "Fists of Fury," between three and five percent of the budget for the low-cost productions goes to buy innumerable half-gallon plastic bottles of sticky artificial blood.

In the 1960s the Hong Kong studios, mainly Shaw Brothers and the Cathay Organization, were producing more than two hundred features annually, mostly in Cantonese.

Then, about 1967, new equipment was brought in and, to widen the market in South Asia, the films were made in Mandarin language. Now almost all films are made in Mandarin.

Shaw Brothers remains the top producer, turning out forty features a year, and Cathay's studio is out of business. Their facilities have been taken over by Raymond Chow and Golden Harvest, almost all formerly Shaw Brothers people, who since 1970 have come on like gangbusters, specializing in action-violence films.

The real story of the Hong Kong film industry, then, is exploitation. Actors, actresses, cameramen, carpenters, grips and gaffers are systematically ripped off by a few extremely wealthy studio heads.

To fully educate myself, I went to visit Run Run Shaw at the Shaw Brothers studio in Hong Kong's New Territory and about forty miles from the center of the Kowloon business district.

Shaw is a slim, intense, graying, highly polished man who could play the part of an Oriental trader in a B-thriller, and whose real-life story is twice as interesting as anything Hollywood's dream merchants ever conjured up.

In fact, Shaw has more power than Zanuck, Mayer, Goldwyn and Warner ever dreamed of at the height of their empire building.

Most of his contract players and many administrators live on the lot in cement block dormitories or hostels and work for low wages under primitive conditions on long-term contracts. If that sounds uninviting, consider this: not only is there an eager waiting list willing to ink such deals, but Shaw actually gets extras to pay for the privilege of being part of his company by enrolling them in the company acting school for a modest fee.

Only one out of fifty acting students gets a contract. Once signed, players work up to six years for $50 per week or so, without any real unions, insurance, fringe or medical benefits. Extras must brown-bag their own lunch and provide their own transport to location shootings.

Recently, one of the growing legion of free-lance European extras was wired with charges that were to go off making her appear to be shot, a common Hollywood practice. The prop man did his job poorly, however, and the charges went off in reverse, shooting tiny bits of shrapnel into the girl's body.

Although Shaw Brothers studio covers forty-six acres, has fifteen hundred employees, ten sound stages and sixteen permanent sets, it doesn't have any resident medical personnel or ambulance. In fact, on this particular day, the first-aid kit was discovered empty.

Another girl on the set had some medical training and closed her wounds so the extra could be driven at high speed to a hospital, a half hour away.

Run Run Shaw's office is carefully, frugally furnished, with tasteful modern Chinese art. There is a solid feeling to the room, although it is hardly friendly.

Shaw's presence is insignificant behind the big desk, but when he speaks and splashes his elbows on the leather arms of his chair he exhibits a certain detached command. There is a touch of repressed contempt for a Western journalist whose Hong Kong tape recorder keeps failing to work.

The legend of the fabulous Shaw Brothers, whose empire has tentacles all over Asia, dates back to the early Twenties in the Northern Chinese city of Shanghai, then famed for its international intrigue and action. In 1923, the story goes, the four sons of a wealthy Shanghai businessman, their fortune having gone sour, met to decide whether to sell the family house or the family movie theater. They decided to sell the house and continue showing silent films in the theater, which also became their home.

Then the eldest brother Runjy (Run Run is youngest) wrote a play and, just to see how it would go, the brothers decided to put it on in their theater. The play was called "Man from Shensi," a melodrama about an outlaw who helps the poor. On the first night the hero leaped into the air and fell right through some rotten boards in the stage floor. The audience, thinking it was all part of the show, roared with appreciative laughter and applauded wildly. The "accident" became a permanent part of the show, and the show became a smash hit.

The biggest thing in film in Shanghai at the time was the newly arrived American silents, including Charlie Chaplin, and people lined up for blocks to get a seat. The Shaw Brothers, on another lark, decided to invest in a movie camera to record "Man from Shensi" and see if people would accept it as a film. After a five-minute rundown from the camera salesman on how it was done, they brought the hand-crank camera home. Run Run Shaw was chosen to crank the camera because he had the steadiest hand.

By day they filmed and by evening they presented "Man from Shensi" on stage. What they created has come to be called the first Chinese film, and became a huge commercial success. The film cost the Shaw Brothers about $400 to make and grossed thousands. It didn't take much success to firmly plant the idea in the brothers' heads that a market of five hundred million Chinese held vast potential. The only problem was the totally unstable political situation in China at the time. Foreigners took concessions, guerrilla armies roamed looting and pillaging almost at will during certain periods. And where armies failed to wreak ruin, it seemed natural disaster was sure to do the job.

The final blow was the rise of the warlords in China, with their bullyboy private armies. These soldiers gate-crashed the theaters padding their pistols for complimentary tickets. Like some modern action movie-goers they hooted and howled once inside the theaters and ripped up seats and threw things at the screen.

So, in 1925, as the legend goes, Number Three Son Runme Shaw, who now lives a multi-millionaire's existence of business and philanthropy in Singapore, tucked a few films under his arm and headed south.

The young Shaw combed the Malay Peninsula looking for theaters to show his films, but there was none, so he did the only thing he could, he built his own. In the first years Runme Shaw and later his brothers scraped up enough capital to build movie houses in Singapore, Kuala Lumpur, Penang and Ipoh.

Run Run arrived in Singapore in 1926, and they lived in the back of the Shaw office in a four-story building in a crowded section of the port city. Run

Run slept wedged among the film cans, after working all day, existing on a few bowls of rice and soup. "In those days," said Run Run, "show business was not regarded by respectable Chinese as a particularly respectable occupation."

The depression arrived worldwide in the early 1930s and took its toll in South Asia. Tin and rubber prices fell to disastrously low levels, putting millions out of work and sounding what seemed a death knell to the theater business. Run Run suggested the Shaws import foreign "talkies," but everyone told him he was out of his mind. He insisted, however, and the brothers not only rebounded, they made their fortune.

The first sound projector they imported had to be carried around from theater to theater, with Run Run on one side and Runme on the other side of "our money machine."

Having proved there was a lucrative market for "talkies," the Shaws produced Asia's first sound picture in their newly opened Hong Kong studio in 1936, "White Golden Dragon."

With all their new capital and new talking films, the Shaw Brothers bought a second sound projector and headed out, dividing Malaya between them. Run Run went south and Runme went north. In towns or villages along the Malay Peninsula, each would set up his projector and, poof, instant theater. Some of the audiences had never even heard of movies before, and all were delighted.

Much of the Shaws' profits, as they traveled, were invested in local real estate which, over the years, has spiraled in value.

By 1938 the Shaw Brothers had seventy-nine theaters all over Southeast Asia and were producing Chinese films in both Singapore and Hong Kong.

Then, in 1941, the Japanese overran Asia.

Never among those caught napping, the Shaws foresaw the coming of a night of terror and quickly turned all their considerable liquid assets into jewels which, according to legend, they hid in their own backyard.

When the Japanese arrived, they showed no mercy and the Shaws, like so many others, lost all visible assets. All their estates were confiscated and almost all their theaters leveled. Their equipment was stolen and most of their film prints went up in flame.

Unlike most other refugees, after the war the Shaws dug up their buried treasure and quickly rebounded once again. Run Run later told an interviewer, "The pearls were a little brown, the watches rusty, the bank notes mildewed, but the gold was nice and yellow. The diamonds, sapphires and emeralds were in excellent form. We were still rich."

There was little entertainment and little equipment right after the war in Asia, but what there was the Shaws quickly acquired. Using their experience and capital, the Shaws soon had a lock on the production and distribution of films throughout Asia, a hold they kept in South Asia through the present day.

Shaw Brothers Ltd. was incorporated in Singapore in 1958, as the movie business grew side by side with the family's many outside investments. These include, besides extensive real estate holdings, a chain of amusement parks, banks, an insurance company, a family foundation in Singapore, and the movie houses. At last count the Shaws owned one hundred forty movie houses, but actually booked for more like five hundred (including theaters in the Chinatowns of San Francisco, New York, Los Angeles and Honolulu).

Around 1958 Run Run Shaw became dissatisfied with the quality of films the brothers' film factory was producing. Like the rest of the Asian producers, the Shaws were making quickies on a low budget, in black and white. As Runme oversaw a fantastic program of expansion, a theater a month for two years, Run Run headed for Hong Kong where he was to build Asia's largest, most complete dream factory.

"We wanted to revolutionize Chinese films," says

Run Run Shaw. He traveled to the States and absorbed every aspect of Hollywood he could discover. On his return, against all sensible advice, Run Run decided to make his epic. He chose a Chinese classical story and staked what was then a massive $100,000 on the project. The story goes that Shaw handed the money to his director and said, "Now go do it." Whatever the truth, the film, "Kingdom and the Beauty," went on to huge success and has become a classic among Chinese films. The film's star was the legendary Lin Dai.

In 1960 Run Run Shaw broke ground on his big studio in Hong Kong's Clear Water Bay area. The studio cost an estimated $5 million, dwarfing any facility anywhere outside Western Europe and the United States.

Shaw Brothers (Hong Kong), the film company alone, went public in 1971, issuing $8.3 million in shares representing twenty-five percent of the company.

"We want the public to have a piece of our profits," Run Run Shaw told the local papers at the time. "This is a public business. We cater to hundreds of thousands of people each day, and we want these people to have more than a passing interest in us, our work and our movies."

"Shaw Bros. (Hong Kong) Ltd.," reported George V. Liu of the Asian News Service, "estimated conservatively to be worth U.S. $35 million today (1971), is just one company in the Shaw financial empire, which encompasses thirty-six firms in Singapore and Malaysia, chains of theaters in Hong Kong and Southeast Asia and a variety of real estate and other interests."

The entire family fortune has been conservatively estimated at around $200 million; and even as much as one billion dollars.

Profits for the film company in 1971 were in excess of $3 million, and each year since has gotten significantly better.

Run Run Shaw has been known to begin and end a two-hour conversation by asking quite directly, "What's in it for me?" He doesn't like to talk about the low wages and primitive conditions in his industry, brushing them aside with a wave of his frail hand; but he can be quite vocal about the sudden success films featuring martial arts have been enjoying around the world.

Shaw sees the kung fu film as a logical result of the public's insatiable demand for action and adventure. He says after the war films of the Forties, the Fifties played out the westerns, which were followed by the Hercules-and-Bible-sandal epics of the early Sixties, mostly from Italy. These were succeeded by the James Bond technical-electrical flicks, which have now been succeeded by gangster films and the kung fu flicks.

Shaw's films propagandize no political views or radical social ideas. He says simply, "If they want violence, we give them violence. If they want sex, we give them sex. Whatever the audience wants, we will give them."

Shaw's studio, set in a lush paradise valley between green hills and twisting inland seas, is a hive of continuous activity. An average of seven features are always in production, sharing the sound stages and dubbing rooms on three shifts per day.

On one end of the facility is a make-believe pagoda, an ancient Cantonese bridge, and a Japanese-style concentration camp used recently to film a gross sex-adventure that will soon be released in the United States. The camp has been used in a dozen films in the past two years.

Across the lot is an engine shop, a re-creation of a 1915 Chinese general's mansion, and a small city of other sets from various eras of Eastern history. There are whole streets of Chinese architectural facades, an Eastern version of the western town backlots still to be found on Universal's or Paramount's lots in Hollywood.

Off in another corner is Run Run Shaw's party house where lavish galas are thrown on almost any pretense, from the opening of a film to the completion of a new sound stage. While the Shaw Brothers go in for only a minimum of Western-style public relations, they go in for a maximum of Eastern-style partying with miles of tables laden with gourmet specialties.

To a side of the party house, workmen are building Babylonian gardens, not for a film, but for Run Run to stroll in.

Only ten minutes away is Run Run Shaw's favorite of his several houses, easily reached in any of his several Rolls-Royces. Shaw also has houses on several islands near Hong Kong for summer retreats when city dwellers and contract players are suffering the humid, intense South Asia summer.

Hong Kong journalist John Luff describes Run Run Shaw's life style:

"His day begins at seven o'clock. For half an hour at his rising he is strictly undisturbed as he goes through the motions of Chinese boxing exercises (Tai Chi Chuan). Then he reads his papers right through breakfast and at nine o'clock sharp, the boss is at his desk down on the third floor.

"The mail piles high. He takes two hours to go through it, jotting down instructions on tiny memo sheets for his executives to handle. By eleven o'clock he is ready for the stream of callers. They are the directors, scriptwriters, theater managers and business executives. There are the movie stars as well as the scores of officers to confer with and advise in the sprawling administrative department. Meanwhile, there are the telephone calls which follow one on the other.

"In the afternoon the head of the Shaw Organization slips quietly into the preview room for a look at the latest rushes. More people are waiting for him, some of them foreign film executives visiting town. As often as he is able to, he rushes off to the studio to see how things are going with the latest productions.

His evenings are taken up with social engagements, mostly business. Often, he returns, still in black tie, to his desk and works through the night."

Shaw is quoted by interviewer John Hardie of the *China Star* as caring little about all the beautiful actresses he comes in contact with. In fact, he professes to enjoy his role as "father figure."

"I am very happy with my wife," says Shaw. "I have two sons who have graduated from Oxford, and I have two daughters who have graduated from Bryn Mawr, outside Philadelphia. I have seven grandchildren. I have a happy family.

"My only regret is that I don't have more time to spend with my grandchildren. Some are in Honolulu, some in Singapore, and two are in Hong Kong.

"Hong Kong is one of the few spots in the world where the movie industry is still flourishing," continues Shaw. "In Hollywood, Japan and Europe, the industry is not doing so well. Maybe this is due to labor costs or television.

"The stars are constantly demanding more money. All this is against us. We have to try new ideas all the time to improve our production."

Shaw told another interviewer, Shelia Gibbs, he had no interest at all in acting himself. "I'm no actor, and I never could be. I'm more interested in developing actors—training them, and then seeing the results of their studies on the screen.

"We have a very efficient acting school at Movie Town (the common name for Shaw Brothers studio), and as well as bringing up a good crop of actors and actresses, we train singers and dancers, too—there's no shortage of talent."

Shaw told Sheila Gibbs there is a problem with the sudden fame thrust on some actors and actresses. "There have been a number of suicides and such-like over the years. There is a great problem in that you get ordinary people, and, suddenly, they're famous. Fans hound them, they become larger than life, and they sometimes lose their balance.

"The emotional strain involved in changing from a nobody into a film star is something terrible. Their income, their identity, everything changes for them.

"I must say I always try to be available to assist if anything looks like it is happening to any of our stars.

"Everything comes in crazes," Shaw continues, "and we must produce what the people want to see. At the moment they want the excitement of action and bloodthirstiness—it takes them out of themselves, and relieves the monotony of their own lives. So we produce what the audience wants. But this will pass quite soon . . .

"We have been accused in the Chinese film-making industry of stealing themes from films produced by other countries. But this is not so—I mean, there must be some similarities between films anyway because there are only so many basic themes one can work on: love, hate, war, boy-meets-girl, murder, theft, divorce, spy films and spoofs. So somewhere along the track we must use some of these.

"Actually, the modern trend in film-making has been somewhat taxing on the Chinese actors and actresses. Five years ago, for instance, it was hard work for them to kiss on screen. Now, with the trend toward nude love-making scenes in films—well, it's going to be hard on them.

"One thing I'll say, though, our actors and actresses learn fast. If it's got to be done, and there's money and stardom involved, they certainly learn fast.

"I don't have time to be a playboy," says Shaw who has ten villas across Asia and a fleet of Rolls-Royces and Lincolns. "My houses are a convenience, the cars a luxury I can afford, and I can only drive one of them at a time anyway, so I like a change—and as for the girls, well, as a film-maker, it's hard for me not to be anywhere that my stars are not.

"Whenever photographers are around, when I'm in public, it's usually a promotion to go with a film, which naturally includes the stars who are involved with the film.

"I am so involved with my work and my work is my pleasure. Occasionally, when I have time, I do play a game of golf.

"When I really get to the stage where I'm worn out with work, then I jet off somewhere, like Australia. I particularly like Australia. It has a great potential for a film industry—it's the country of the future."

Shaw is almost guaranteed a profit on all of his films because of his distribution system. The Mandarin film circuit, first-run, snakes through Hong Kong, Singapore, Indonesia, Malaysia, Taiwan and Thailand, and covers some of Vietnam and Burma.

What Run Run Shaw puts in the pipe comes out on five hundred screens. If it is any good at all, it makes money.

What about TV? In most places it is only a minor factor. Even where it is a threat, Shaw says it did cause a slight dip in attendance for a couple of years when first popularized, but has since lost its effect. "I believe," he says, "people like to see a proper movie rather than a movie on a small box."

Instead of a star system, with its built-in salary escalations, Shaw uses the rent-a-star system. He features his best players in only one or two films a year to keep their price low, while those he can exploit may be seen in fifteen or twenty films in a year.

One seventeen-year-old girl on long-term contract for about $110 per week had nine leading roles in major features in ten months.

Shaw is currently refurbishing his studio and gearing up for a wave of coproductions that have resulted from new interest in the Hong Kong industry generated by the martial arts boom.

Shaw and Italian director Gianfranco Parolini, for instance, are about to turn out what has been billed in the Hong Kong press as "spaghetti kung fu."

"After all," points out a Hong Kong journalist, "it

was the Chinese who introduced noodles to Italians."

The film will incorporate comedy, violence, slap-stick, kung fu and adventure, on a low budget with quickie distribution.

Shaw is weighing coproduction offers and distribution deals from almost every major American studio, although mostly not for films featuring martial arts.

Run Run Shaw says the kung fu movie craze is on the wane. He has no interest in any more martial arts films unless they have an additional gimmick, like the comic Italian production.

One of Shaw's producers for a number of years was Raymond Chow, who split off in 1970 to form Golden Harvest taking with him some of Shaw Brothers' key people.

Chow's studio believes there are a few punches and kicks left in the martial arts wave, but with the death of Bruce Lee it is beginning to look like he is wrong and Shaw is right.

Shaw and Chow are bitter enemies who would go out of their way to do each other evil.

Now that the Western film-makers have discovered Hong Kong, where even a feature with Hollywood markings like Lee's "Enter the Dragon" for Warner Brothers can be done for a paltry half million, the battle of Hong Kong is just beginning.

Bruce Lee was the human cannonball fired to announce that the Hong Kong film industry has joined the world.

"You know," concludes Run Run Shaw, "I am rather tired of people saying, 'Are you trying to challenge Hollywood?' I really feel we have something quite different and equally as good as Hollywood has to offer."

6

The Dragon Breathes Fire

"Give me a place to stand and I will move the world."

—Archimedes

There are ninety-seven cinemas in Hong Kong, with a total seating capacity of 118,355. Attendance figures per population, according to Crown Colony Information Services, are among the highest in the world and amounted to 71,279,000 admissions in 1972. Ticket prices were recently raised on the average film to one dollar.

No one before Bruce Lee filled those 118,355 seats better than he. Several have broken his records, with non-kung fu films, since.

If Lee is easily forgotten in the West, it is because not enough people ever came to know him. Why he has seemingly been quickly forgotten in Hong Kong is a longer, more complex tale that will unfold later.

When he arrived in 1970 with five-year-old son Brandon propped on one shoulder, Bruce Lee was amazed at his reception. Not only was he known, he was in demand. Newspapers wanted interviews. TV wanted him for talk shows. Radio wanted him for guest spots. He was Kato, and he was the hometown hero who had gone to Hollywood and made good.

When "The Green Hornet" ended its one-season run in the American market, it began years of syndication around the world. Nowhere was it more popular than in Hong Kong.

Also, many of Bruce Lee's earlier films, mostly co-starring roles, kept the name Lee Siu Loong (Little Dragon) before the public because they would be run and rerun on the two Chinese television channels in Hong Kong.

Probably the two films best remembered are "Thunder and Rain," a play on film Bruce did when he was sixteen, and "The Long and Winding Road," which starred veteran Chinese actor Ng Choi-fan (who also directed). Also in the latter film with Lee, then fifteen, was actress Pak Yin. This film got special note because it was the first Chinese film in color and wide screen.

After the years of frustration in America, Bruce ate up the affection and good karma awaiting him in Hong Kong. The highlights of his trip were two television appearances he made on late evening talk shows, during which he gave what came to be highly publicized demonstrations of his art. Basically, he did a supercharged version of his tournament demonstration.

"They dangled in the air five one-inch boards," recalled Bruce, "and I sidekicked it and broke four of them."

For dessert the audience got to watch five-year-old Brandon, whom Bruce had begun training in martial arts as soon as he could walk, go through his paces and conclude by breaking in half a board almost as big as he was.

As much as Bruce enjoyed his visit, he had to return to Los Angeles to continue working with his private students who were, by then, paying over $150 per hour for instruction, and to do an episode of the TV series "Longstreet" with James Franciscus, arranged for him by Sterling Silliphant.

The script for the first of four "Longstreets" Bruce eventually did was written mostly by Silliphant. Lee added his own poignant touches, and it was truly memorable for a TV series episode.

The episode was called "The Way of the Intercepting Fist," which is a translation for Jeet Kune Do. Franciscus plays a blind insurance detective in the series. In the opening of the episode he "overhears" a murder, but can't prove to the police he can make a positive identification with his ears alone.

After tracking down the killer, a husky longshoreman, Longstreet decides the way to flush him out is to challenge him to a fight. Lee, who has earlier befriended Longstreet, is asked to train him for the fight.

The show propagates the false image of instant karate, but it also gives Bruce a chance to explain some of the spiritual side of the art.

"You weren't born being able to take apart three men in a matter of seconds," Longstreet says to Lee when the latter has become frustrated teaching his blind pupil.

"I found the cause of my ignorance," replies Lee.

"Well, help me find mine," cajoles Longstreet.

"I cannot teach you," Lee says later on, "I can only help you explore yourself."

When Lee tries to explain the "it" of directness any true karateka must find, Longstreet becomes frustrated.

"You have a quarrelsome mind, Mr. Longstreet," says Lee. "Unless you learn to calm it, you will never hear the world outside.

"You must learn defeat," Lee adds. "Like most people you want to learn to win."

Then, in what seems now a prophetic statement, Lee told Longstreet, "To learn to die is to be liberated from it. When tomorrow comes, you must learn to die and be liberated by it."

Tomorrow comes, and Longstreet takes a lot of punishment from the burly longshoreman he has goaded into fighting him, but, in the end, comes out the victor.

The "Longstreet" producers so liked the episode, they used it as the season's opener during Fall Premiere Week. A number of critics reviewed the show, almost all favorably. Lee had never had a large dose of critics' reactions before, especially raves, and commented to a number of people how pleasant he thought it was.

One critic who had some complaint with Lee's "Longstreet" appearance, however, was Ed Parker. Lee had used a line in the show, one of his favorites, "The usefulness of a cup is in its emptiness."

"From the view of the cup," says Ed Parker, "that is true. From the view of the recipient of the cup, the value is in its fullness. A lot of these philosophical things sound good, but, if you really analyze it, only the cup could agree."

Suddenly Bruce Lee found his cup running over. After "Longstreet" a number of Hollywood studios decided they would like to see more. This little-known Chinese had gotten more fan mail after the first show than James Franciscus.

Warner Brothers then had a show under consideration that was to eventually become the hit TV series "Kung Fu." Bruce was called in and did a round of interviews. He had been developing an idea of his own about a rebel Shao-lin priest who would roam the U.S. Old West, and suddenly here was Warner's telling him that's just what they had on their mind.

The outcome was a major disappointment for Bruce and a brutal loss of face. While Bruce thought the studio was really interested, and began setting his heart on the show, Tom Kuhn, head of Warner Brothers television, says the studio never really took Lee seriously. "We didn't think Bruce could be a weekly television star, which is different from doing one-shot features. Although we knew he wanted it, Bruce Lee was never seriously considered."

Kuhn says Warner's, ABC and the agents felt that Lee's English was not accent-free enough, that he wasn't enough of a name to carry the show, and that he didn't have enough experience.

Linda Weintraub, who was married to Ted Ashley, president of Warner Brothers at the time, says ABC turned down Bruce because they thought he was too short and too Chinese.

Meanwhile the waves from Bruce's trip to Hong Kong were still pounding the shore. A radio interviewer called trans-Pacific to ask if Bruce would entertain any more film offers from the Orient. Sure, replied Lee, if the money and script were right.

The offers flooded in by letter and cable from Hong Kong and Taiwan. Producer Raymond Chow, who had recently formed his Golden Harvest Productions and was in financial trouble, sent the wife of his top director to negotiate directly with Bruce. Mrs. Lo returned home with a signed contract. Bruce Lee would make two films for Golden Harvest for an estimated $10,000 each.

For Bruce the decision was only slightly difficult. Linda Lee recalls that Bruce didn't really want to return to Hong Kong, but after all the frustrations with studios and networks in America, he saw his only real chance to make films with his special imprint was in Hong Kong. It meant wealth and artistic freedom.

"He didn't start anything he didn't finish one hundred percent," recalls Linda Lee. "So he said, 'The heck with Hollywood and thirteen-week contracts.' He liked quality and that meant features. He had a chance to do his will in the film industry in Hong Kong."

"After I signed my contract with Raymond," Bruce recalled for *Fighting Stars Magazine*, "I received a call from a producer in Taiwan. That guy told me to rip up the contract and he'd top Raymond's offer and even take care of any lawsuit for breaking the agreement."

Lee, whose native tongue was Cantonese, said the first thing he did after returning to Hong Kong was go to see all the Mandarin flicks in town. "They were terrible," he recalled later. "Everybody always fighting the same way, and fighting all the time. They were unrealistic, always a lot of overacting. I introduced some new elements, some subtlety, like when I kicked, I really kicked."

Lee also insisted there be less fighting for fighting's sake and more plot, the mental heritage of his years in America.

Robert S. Elegant in his January 1973 *Los Angeles Times* article explained the system well: " 'The simple message is that violence is apparently more appealing than the convoluted sexual and psychological intricacies of the West,' a screenwriter observed.

" 'And let's keep it that way,' a visiting distributor from Caracas added. 'I'm afraid the new karate and boxing films are getting too complicated for my customers. They like the good old simple sword fighting films.'

" . . . 'Basically,' the scriptwriter said, 'almost every really successful movie of the past decade comes down to one theme—revenge. For good reason, we Chinese are today obsessed with revenge. After all, we feel we've been kicked around by foreigners for the past 200 years.'

"But the passion for revenge goes back much further. Confucius himself warned against the passion 2500 years ago. The vendetta was a fixture of Chinese society long before Sicilians and hillbillies adopted the blood feud as an interesting way to pass time. Celluloid plus revenge plus violence equal profits.

"Chinese studios are now under pressure from two of their chief markets—Singapore and Taiwan—to cut down on violence. But the most dynamic producer is not terribly concerned.

"Shanghai-born Raymond Chow, 45, who has made a modern fortune since he went into business for himself less than three years ago, feels that the new emphasis upon unarmed combat, rather than sword fighting, will enable him to satisfy both bloodthirsty audiences and the censors," Elegant reports.

Bruce was sent on location to Thailand with a crew led by rotund, graying director Lo Wei, husband of the woman who had signed Bruce to a two-picture deal.

Lee found the working conditions incredible after

his American experience. He was totally cut off from the world, away from all communications except an occasional letter, with food in short supply and a script outline that was to be filled in as the production moved along. The film's budget was between $85,000 and $100,000, less than an Army training film could be made for in America, and considerably less than a TV network sixty-second commercial would cost to produce in New York.

"He kept writing," recalls Linda Lee, "there's nothing to eat here."

When he came home, he had lost weight, which was always one of his physical problems, but had completed a film that was to make history and smash box-office records, not just on the Mandarin circuit, but in Beirut, Rome, Sydney and Buenos Aires as well.

The plot of the film is crudely simple, but in my opinion that film is the finest acting job of Bruce Lee's career. It is one of the most outstanding examples of sheer animal presence on celluloid ever produced, and I would match it against the best of Clint Eastwood, Steve McQueen or the various James Bonds.

The Mandarin title was "Big Boss." It was released in the United States as "Fists of Fury" and in other parts of the world as "Fists of Glory."

The plot concerns the struggle of Chinese in Bangkok who live in fear of gangsters. Lee takes a job in an ice factory and discovers the place is actually a front for the mob's illegal business.

Through the entire first half of the film, Bruce doesn't throw a punch or a kick against the gangsters. He has made a vow to his family that he will never fight again, after years of rowdy, revengeful problems, and after each loss of face he seethes, holding in the power that seems to make his eyes bulge.

By the time Bruce breaks loose, the audience is practically on its feet begging him to fight. He releases a fury of punches and kicks that instantly establish him as the number-one macho fighting star of kung fu.

The high point of the film, for the action addict, is Lee's one-man battle against more than a dozen racketeers with clubs and knives. He not only wins, but he does it with style.

It is as if, in this film, Bruce didn't really know what he was doing, so he just went out and did a job. He had not intellectualized any ideas about Hong Kong films yet because this was his first film. His battles with director Lo Wei had not yet really begun, although from the start Lee didn't like the director's attitudes or methods. Mostly Bruce didn't like to take orders, especially when he was dead-sure the orders could be improved upon with slightly more effort.

The film made almost a million dollars in Hong Kong alone in its initial run, eclipsing the previous record held by "The Sound of Music." Wherever it opened, the box-office results were the same, the film was a smash.

When Bruce had returned from Bangkok, he found excited secretaries at Golden Harvest waving stacks of telegrams from Paramount at him. While his Kato in "The Green Hornet" series had made him appear a hero to the other actors and actresses in Hong Kong, the extensive Paramount efforts to reach Bruce made him a superstar. For most of them, Hollywood was never-never land, while for Bruce it was a place to find work and frustration.

The telegrams were requests for Bruce to do three more "Longstreet" episodes to follow up the phenomenal response "The Way of the Intercepting Fist" had elicited.

Bruce went back but wasn't happy with the other three episodes. They were not written by Silliphant and didn't showcase either his talents or philosophy properly. In two shows he was no more than a continuing character, a friend of the blind detective, who passes through the scene. His talents were misused, and it just added to his feeling that he would be better off in Hong Kong features than American television.

While he was in Los Angeles, Bruce visited the

Black Belt Magazine offices and shared some of his thoughts on the future of Hong Kong kung fu films.

". . . People like films that are more than just one long, armed hassle," Lee said in the May 1972 issue. "With any luck, I hope to make multi-level films (in Hong Kong)—the kind of movies where you can just watch the surface story if you want, or you can look deeper into it if you feel like it."

Lee described his character in "Fists of Fury" as "a simple straightforward guy. Like, if you told this guy something, he'd believe you. Then when he finally figures out he's been had, he goes animal."

Lee supposedly saw his own future looming ahead of him. He is quoted in a later National General Pictures press release as predicting that American audiences are ready to accept Chinese films. These quotes should be taken with a grain of salt, however, since in all of National General's biographies of Bruce, they claim he had a master's degree from the University of Washington. He never even graduated from there, and never hid that fact. The Hollywood publicity machine has never been noted for accuracy, and they built Bruce to suit their needs, just as they had built Robert Taylor and Errol Flynn and others thirty years earlier.

National General quotes Bruce at the time "Fists of Fury" opened:

"These should do for me what the spaghetti westerns did for Clint Eastwood. There is such an incredible amount of interest in the East since the visit of President Nixon that our films should find ready acceptance in the American market. I think we have what the U.S. public wants—violence and humor. I mean, nobody can take seriously a scene in which a man is stabbed and his intestines come out and yet he picks them up, ties them around his waist and continues the fight. It's almost the kind of humor that the Bond films have."

"Everything is overplayed in Mandarin films," Lee told *Black Belt*. "To make really good ones, you have to use subtlety, and very few people in the business want to risk any money by trying that."

Black Belt concluded the article by adding, "Ever since his reputation put him in the headlines, he has been getting challenges almost daily from publicity-seeking clowns who want to take him on. Bruce laughs them off but admits that it does get annoying constantly listening for footsteps from behind."

7

Hong Kong Heart Throb

"The grandest forms of active force
From Tao come, their only source.
Who can of Tao the nature tell?
Eluding touch, eluding sight,
There are their semblances, all right.
Profound it is, dark and obscure;
Things' essences all there endure.
Those essences the truth enfold
Of what, when seen, shall then be told.
Now it is so, 'twas so of old.
Its name—what passes not away;
So, in their beautiful array,
Things form and never know decay.

"How know I that it is so with all the beauties of existing things? By this (nature of the Tao)."

> —Tao Teh Ching, "The Empty Heart,"
> quoted from *Chinese Mystics*

" 'Fists of Fury' was an important movie for me," Bruce Lee told *Fighting Stars Magazine*, "because I had a starring role for the first time. I felt that I could do a better acting job than in 'Green Hornet' and had more confidence since I just did Paramount's 'Way of the Fist.' I didn't expect 'Fists of Fury' to break any kind of record, but I did expect it to be a money-maker. I realized the potential of the movie when I attended the premiere.

"Bob Baker (from Stockton, California) was in town for a part in the second movie, 'The Chinese

Connection.' He and I sat in the front seats without being noticed. As the movie progressed, we kept looking at the reactions of the fans. They hardly made any noise in the beginning, but at the end they were in frenzy and began clapping and clamoring. Those fans there are emotional. If they don't like the movie, they'll cuss and walk out. When the movie came to an end, Bob, almost in tears, shook my hand and said, 'Boy, am I happy for you.'"

In 1971 Bruce, Linda, Brandon and little Shannon, a recently arrived daughter, moved temporarily back to Hong Kong while Bruce worked on his second film for Chow, "The Chinese Connection."

The second film was done on a backlot in Hong Kong. Bruce, recalls Linda, was growing more and more dissatisfied with Lo Wei, the director. Bruce complained there was really no script, and not even much of an outline, and production techniques and standards were haphazard.

Lo Wei, complained Bruce, simply didn't seem interested in what was going on. "During a tender love scene," says Linda, "Lo Wei might be listening to the dog races on the radio."

Their arguments would eventually erupt into a well-publicized feud.

The plot of "The Chinese Connection" is, of course, revenge. This time the story is set in Shanghai in 1908 where Lee, playing Chen Chen, arrives to attend the funeral of his martial arts school's top teacher, the famous Ho Yuan-chia.

From a broader perspective, the film is notable as the most mindless, violent and realistic (in terms of action) of Lee's films. He comes as close as he ever did on screen to being a mad dog.

From the point of view of his development as an actor, he is flashier, but not much better than in "Fists of Fury"; but his cat-like kiai, or fighting yell, is fully developed.

In kung fu the kiai serves three purposes. It frightens the opponent, tenses the body so the fighter can receive an unexpected blow without excessive damage, and aids, karate men say, in "gripping" the body in such a way that they get the use of internal, as well as external, energy flows. In other words, it is a way to supercharge a burst of energy. To find Tao.

Lee's distinctive kiai is almost like the cry of a cat or a fighting bird. It was specially developed for the screen, since none of his former students whom I reached remember Bruce working out and using such sounds. Usually Bruce did his exercises either remaining silent or saying specific, verbal things.

"The Chinese Connection" is also the film where Bruce became a hero for downtrodden Chinese. Let me explain the plot more fully; then you will better understand why. Keep in mind the bitter traditional rivalry between the Chinese and the Japanese. It is comparable to the Greek-Turk conflict, or Catholic-Protestant rivalry in Northern Ireland, in many ways.

A few days after Chen Chen arrives in turn-of-the-century Shanghai for the funeral of his old master, a tablet bearing the inscription, "The Sick Nation of Eastern Asia" is delivered to the Ching Wu School (a Chinese boxing club) by Hun En, a Chinese who works for the Japanese Martial Arts Association. Challenges are normal between boxing clubs, but this inscription is an insult to the Chinese people. Chen is angered, so he immediately goes to the Japanese club and singlehandedly beats up the entire membership.

The Japanese are the big political power in town and Nin Mu, the Japanese Association president, is furious. He demands Chen be turned over to his club within three days for arrest. Chen's buddies send him into hiding, and as he reluctantly goes, he discovers Hun En congratulating the cook, a Japanese spy, on his success in poisoning the school's old master.

Chen makes Hun En confess, kills him and hangs his body from a post. The Japanese again demand Chen Chen's arrest.

The Chinese school's two top fighters go off to consult with Chen in a graveyard, and while they are all away, the Japanese show up with a mercenary, a Russian boxer, and beat the devil out of the Chinese and wreck their school.

Chen avenges this with a challenge to the top Japanese and the paid Russian and beats the heck out of them.

When Chen returns to his school, he finds the angry members ready to go attack the Japanese all over again. They are about to march when the Japanese leader shows up with the police and says the whole school will be held responsible unless Chen is handed over.

Chen, hiding on the upper floor, overhears and surrenders to the Shanghai chief of police with the promise his pals will be spared and his school's honor preserved.

Four percent of the film's budget of under $100,000 went to buy gallons of artificial blood.

There aren't really any great emotional displays or intense dialogues in the film, just a lot of sheer action. Of all Lee's films, it gave the Mandarin audience the most of what they wanted.

"At the close of a day's shooting," a production release notes, "a typical set looks like a front-line dressing station after a major battle. We Chinese are a violent people—and that's what audiences want."

The Mandarin audience nicknamed Bruce, roughly translated, "The Man with Three Legs." They were awed by his quick three kick—left, right, left, in barely a twinkling of the eye. Young men wanted to imitate him, and young girls wanted to marry him. He was an important star, and he was Chinese. Imagine how the American Indians would feel if one of their own was suddenly as popular as Steve McQueen. His faults could be overlooked because his future as a spokesman, and simply as a hero to identify with, was so bright.

Later on, after Bruce's death, it was the deflation of this false image that helped tarnish Bruce's place in history; but I will get to that in time.

At that moment Bruce seemed to have all he had

ever dreamed of, except one thing: a film that would be a smash in America and avenge his loss of face at the hands of ABC television.

Bruce also complained bitterly that he had lost his privacy. He couldn't go anywhere in Hong Kong without being flooded by fans or by martial arts challenges. In the dark of a movie theater the usherette would come up, flash a light in his face and ask for an autograph. In restaurants his soup would grow cold while everyone, from cooks to customers, lined up for autographs or simply a glimpse. His face was on countless magazines. Golden Harvest produces numbers of movie magazines and, during his time, Bruce was in full color on the cover of every one of them.

Lee told *Fighting Stars Magazine* that he avoided most social gatherings. "I'm not that type of cat. I don't drink or smoke and those events are many times senseless. I don't like to wear stuffy clothes and be at places where everyone is trying to impress each other. Now, I'm not saying I'm modest. I rather like to be around a few friends and talk informally about such things as boxing and the martial arts.

"Now I understand why stars like Steve (McQueen) and Big Lew (Kareem Jabbar) avoid public places. In the beginning I didn't mind all the publicity I was getting. But soon it got to be a headache answering the same questions over and over again, posing for photos and forcing a smile."

Linda laughs bitterly these days when reminded of all the sordid stories about Bruce that used to be printed in the Hong Kong press. Anytime he had his picture taken with an actress, one of the many Hong Kong scandal sheets was sure to concoct a story about Bruce having an affair with the girl.

"Bruce's favorite evening was staying home and working and studying," says Linda. "He wanted to improve the standards of Chinese movies. He wanted to educate audiences, make them more sophisticated, but he knew it had to be done by degrees.

"He ran each day he was working. His favorite

time to exercise was in the late afternoon. He never stopped stretching . . . if he was just watching television, he was always stretching. 'I've got to keep limber,' he would say. He was always improving himself.

"It was inspiring because he was a man who developed his body to such an extent it made me feel bad to be flabby around him.

"He was superconscious of his body. He had to be to do the stuff he did."

Linda says Bruce brought cases of health foods and high-protein drinks from the States because he could not find similar preparations in Hong Kong. He had a problem with undesirable weight loss and several times a day would have either his special protein or vegetable drink. When he was working, Linda would make him a large thermos to sip between scenes.

The protein drink included Real Blair Protein Powder, powdered milk made with ice water, eggs and their shells, vegetable oil, peanut flour and sometimes bananas. Even a touch of peanut butter occasionally.

Bruce Lee's vegetable drink, prepared with an electric juicer, included carrots, celery and apples.

Linda Weintraub, a friend of Bruce's in Los Angeles, recalls he wouldn't drink coffee and tea, or eat baked goods if he thought they were made with chemicals or preservatives.

Bruce also drank a mix of orange juice, honey water and some Chinese herbs occasionally. Linda Lee recalls she didn't like the taste, but Bruce would tell her it was good for her.

In August 1972 Bruce and Linda, with their two children, and servants Wu Ngan and his wife, plus several dogs and cats, moved into a spacious eleven-room house in the Kowloon side of Hong Kong. The house had a walled-off yard and space for a complete gym Bruce planned to install but was never able to finish.

In the long driveway, hidden by the surrounding walls, was Bruce's Mercedes 350 SL, successor to his red Porsche in California. Bruce loved flashy cars and drove them like a madman, recalls Linda Lee. Shortly before his death he had also ordered a brand new gold Rolls-Royce. He died before it could be delivered to Hong Kong.

The furnishings in Bruce and Linda's home were a mix of Western and Chinese modern, in beaming bright colors, and carefully collected pieces of Chinese art. Bruce had an extensive collection of Chinese weapons he loved to display and demonstrate.

One whole room was given over to housing Bruce's library of books on the fighting arts, not just kung fu, but all styles. Fred Weintraub, coproducer of "Enter the Dragon," recalls one night he and Bruce Lee were having dinner with Senator John Tunney of California in Los Angeles. The conversation became a comparison of kung fu and boxing techniques. "Bruce came out and said he had read two books that John Tunney's father, Gene Tunney, had written," says Weintraub. "None of us even knew of their existence. And John Tunney turned around and said, 'You're the only one in the world who knows he even wrote them.'

"But that was Bruce. He could talk about Zen, Islam, Buddhism . . . He may not have believed in God, but he was deeply spiritual in the Zen sense," says Weintraub.

"I've never seen anybody with the totality of mental and physical efforts and that's what jumps out at you from the screen. That's why even in his first crudely made films in Hong Kong, the force transcends. The vitality, the life force was just staggering."

Bruce's younger brother Robert Li says that if you asked Bruce about religion he would tell you, "I don't believe in anything. I believe in sleeping."

Did Bruce believe in God? "To be perfectly frank," he told me in 1972, "I really do not."

"He believed man is a self-made product," says Linda Lee. "If there is a God, he is within. You don't ask God to give you things, you depend on God for inner theme.

"Bruce believed religions divide people, just as styles (in kung fu) divide people. What works, works . . . If all the religions of the world were one, the world would be united in brotherhood."

In the Western tradition, teaches Alan Watts, God is someone on a large gold throne who shoots thunderbolts and creates people from dirt and ribs.

In the Eastern tradition, God came down and became man. Man is God and God is man. One does not pray to such a god for impossible desires to be fulfilled. One looks to such a god for a philosophy that will provide inner calm so that the chaos all around doesn't matter so much.

Bruce Lee was raised in the Eastern tradition and believed the way to get things accomplished was to do them. The way to be capable of doing them was to be one, both spiritually and physically.

Ultimately Lee was a fatalist. "Where fate unites," said the Chinese philosopher Shuei Hu Chuan, "a thousand miles put not asunder; where fate sunders, nearness does not unite."

Of course, the more Bruce Lee came to be one with his philosophy, the harder his friends found it to reach him. Sterling Silliphant recalls with a touch of bitterness Bruce's reaction when he called him in Hong Kong with what he thought was good news. Silliphant had been signed to write the script for a new Irwin Allen (producer of "The Poseidon Adventure") film at Twentieth Century-Fox, and as part of the deal had gotten a commitment from them to do "The Silent Flute" the way Coburn wanted it done.

"I thought," recalls Silliphant, "I was close to Bruce and all I'd have to do was call, and he'd agree. I was amazed at his reaction. He said he didn't think we could afford him anymore.

"He said, 'Why should I carry Coburn on my shoulders?' It reminded me of the problems in India, his ego needs, and in a way I guess it was his way of retribution for whatever slights he felt on that trip.

"He said, 'I understand you are studying Japanese

karate. How could you do that?' He called it an act of betrayal.

" 'You left me,' I told him, 'what was I supposed to do?'

"Bruce wanted to know," continues Silliphant, "if we were going to continue without him. I said we were. He wanted to know where we could find anyone to replace him, to play five parts. I told him we would get five different actors.

"Then Jim Coburn flew with Elmo Williams (Twentieth Century-Fox producer) to meet with Bruce and to make a firm offer and Bruce just gave Jimmy some shit. Jim doesn't know Bruce said, 'I won't carry Jim on my shoulders.' He won't know it until he reads your book."

Linda Lee says Bruce was no longer willing to accept any role, unless he was the lead.

As Bruce's success grew, his boyish cockiness grew into institutionalized ego. It drove him toward perfection and made him great, but it also made him increasingly difficult for everyone except Linda to live with.

Bruce used to like to tell a story that gave birth to his expression, "The value of a teacup is in its emptiness."

"A learned man once went to a Zen teacher," Bruce wrote in *Black Belt* in September 1971, "to inquire about Zen. As the Zen teacher explained, the learned man would frequently interrupt him with remarks like, 'Oh yes, we have that, too . . .' and so on.

"Finally the Zen teacher stopped talking and began to serve tea to the learned man. He poured the cup full, then kept pouring until the cup overflowed.

" 'Enough!' the learned man once more interrupted. 'No more can go into the cup!'

" 'Indeed, I see,' answered the Zen teacher. 'If you do not first empty your cup, how can you taste my cup of tea?' "

Bruce quickly overfilled his cup with his Hong Kong success, at least on a public level. In private, with

Linda, he continued to practice, study and worry; but in public he grew increasingly intolerant of criticism, and particularly of anyone who professed other styles or philosophies than his own.

Bruce Lee's message was that styles and religions divide people. His way, quite often, of interjecting his message was ultimately even more divisive.

He could never quite forgive the world for lacking his native talent. If you have watched his films closely, you have probably noticed that when Bruce hits, his mouth opens in a circle of accomplishment and stretches quickly into a cruel, satisfied twist. Bruce's single interest was to win, and that is what he taught his students, that is what he insisted on in his films, and that is what gave him his greatest joy. Yet like the teacup story, this joy of excess and need to always win, too, went against much of what he professed.

Lee told James Franciscus on his first "Longstreet" appearance, "You must learn defeat. Like most people you want to learn to win."

"To learn to die is to be liberated from it. When tomorrow comes, you must learn to die and be liberated by it."

For Bruce Lee, as for most of us, it was easier to have a philosophy than to live by it.

An early picture of Bruce Lee, taken in Hong Kong. *(Courtesy of Linda Lee)*

Bruce in his school uniform in Hong Kong, about 14 years old. *(Courtesy of Linda Lee)*

Bruce with his first martial arts instructor, Yip Man, who teaches the Wing Chun style of kung fu in Hong Kong. *(Courtesy of Linda Lee)*

The Cha-Cha Champ of Hong Kong, 1958. *(Courtesy of Linda Lee)*

Bruce's mother and father, Mr. and Mrs. Lee Hoi Chuen. *(Courtesy of Linda Lee)*

Bruce in his first
starring role, at age 17,
in "The Orphan,"
a 1958 film about juvenile
delinquents in Hong Kong.
(Courtesy of Linda Lee)

Bruce, as a boy, in
an early Cantonese film.
(Courtesy of Linda Lee)

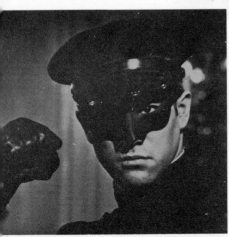

Bruce as Kato in the
1965 television series,
"The Green Hornet."
*(Courtesy of
20th Century-Fox)*

A news photographer caught Linda and Bruce in action during a 1966 Christmas visit to Seattle. *(Photograph by The Seattle Times)*

Bruce Lee in scene from his breakthrough smash hit, "Fists of Fury," made by Golden Harvest Studios. *(Courtesy of National General Pictures)*

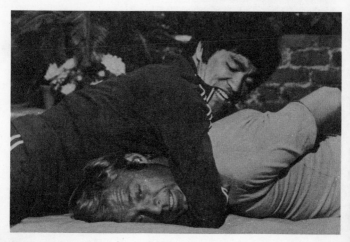

Bruce and his son
Brandon, at age 4,
work out together under
the California sunshine.
Brandon already had
his yellow belt in
judo and karate.
*(Photo by
Linda Weintraub)*

Bruce and Linda Lee
in a 1969 love portrait
in Linda Weintraub's
backyard in Beverly
Hills, California.
*(Photo by
Linda Weintraub)*

Lee teaches a blind insurance investigator, played by
James Franciscus, a fine point of Jeet Kune Do, on
"Longstreet." This was the series' premiere episode for
the 1970 TV season. *(Photo of Bruce Lee and James Franciscus
© Paramount Pictures Corp. All rights reserved.)*

Bruce Lee stars in "The Chinese Connection," his second film for Golden Harvest Studios of Hong Kong. *(Courtesy of National General Pictures)*

Bruce and Nora Miao share a tender moment in "The Chinese Connection." *(Courtesy of National General Pictures)*

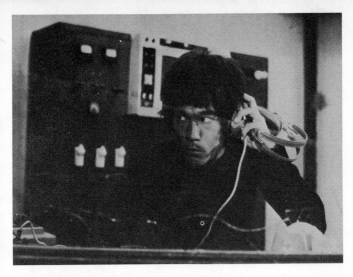

Bruce Lee in "Enter The Dragon," a 1973 release by
Warner Brothers that will eventually gross
an estimated $18 million worldwide.
(Courtesy of Warner Bros. Inc.)

Jim Kelly, hanging, gets an acid bath in a scene from "Enter The Dragon" *(Courtesy of Warner Bros. Inc.)*

Bruce gets advice on the set of "Enter The Dragon" from coproducer Fred Weintraub. *(Courtesy of Warner Bros. Inc.)*

Bruce gives the brothers' handshake to Golden Harvest's president and executive producer Raymond Chow at a Hong Kong film premiere in 1972. *(Courtesy of Linda Lee)*

Bruce works out with Kareem Abdul Jabbar in a scene from the film "Game of Death," which was never completed or released. *(Courtesy of Golden Harvest Studios, Hong Kong)*

Bruce visits the set of "When Tae Kwan Do Strikes." *(l to r)* Bruce Lee, Angela Mao-ying, and Chuck Norris, famed California karate instructor and co-star of "The Way of The Dragon." *(Courtesy of Golden Harvest Studios, Hong Kong)*

Angela Mao-ying commits suicide in "Enter The Dragon" rather than submit to the will of a gang of bullies. *(Courtesy of Warner Bros. Inc.)*

These scenes of an Oriental town are actually movie sets at the Shaw Bros. Studio in Hong Kong's New Territories. *(Photos by Frank Price of Farkas Studio, Hong Kong)*

Mr. Run Run Shaw at his desk in the offices
of Shaw Bros. Studio. *(Photo by
Frank Price of Farkas Studio, Hong Kong)*

The Lees return to Seattle after
Bruce's death. In the living room
of their Bellevue, Washington, home
are Shannon, Linda, and Brandon Lee.
(Photo by Pete Liddell, November 1973)

Among the pall bearers at Bruce Lee's
funeral in Seattle are actors James Coburn (left)
and Steve McQueen (right), both
former martial arts pupils of Bruce Lee.
(Photograph by The Seattle Times, July 30, 1973)

Garlands and wreaths from friends in Seattle,
July 30, 1973. The streamers from the flowers offer
Buddhist blessings for the soul of a fallen hero.
Lee was buried on a hill at Lake View Cemetery
in Seattle. *(Wide World Photos)*

8

Dragons Too Grow Weary

"The rhythm of karate and its bodily movement in relation to the environment is an imitation of the original life-and-death struggle which gave impetus to the behavior pattern. Thus, the impulse is retained (along with the need to face death). But the end— kill or be killed in the life-and-death struggle—is transcended through the symbolic nature of karate practice. In this way, the karate artist learns to overcome his fear of death."

—Paul Leonard Turse, Jr., Ph.D.,
quoted from *Black Belt*,
April 1972

"The Chinese Connection" broke all the box-office records of "Fists of Fury." It grossed almost a million dollars in Hong Kong alone.

"In Singapore," reported *Fighting Stars Magazine*, "scalpers were getting $45 for a $2 ticket. On opening night hundreds of movie patrons rushed to the theater and caused such a traffic jam that they had to suspend showing the movie for a week until the authorities found a way to resolve the problem. This was the first time in Singapore history that a movie caused such a jam."

"Fists of Fury" and "The Chinese Connection," distributed in the U.S. by National General, grossed an amazing $6 million between them in the United States during their first run ("The Chinese Connection" amounted to the larger part, $3.3 million).

One Hong Kong newspaper editorialized, "At last, here in Hong Kong, we have a performer with the wit and intelligence to distinguish between a sprocketed silk purse and a celluloid sow's ear . . . off screen Li (as they chose to spell it) is clearly an asset amid a local film industry bankrupt in everything but quantity."

An interviewer asked Lee if he was a superhero in his films. "I don't play the superhero," he answered. "But the audience wants to make me one. I don't always play the same kind of role. Each role is different, although when I fight, I come out the same—like an animal.

"I never depend solely on my fighting skill to fulfill any of my film roles, although the audiences in Southeast Asia seem to think so. I believe it is more my personality and the expression of my body and myself. I am not acting. I am just doing my thing. When somebody tries to mimic my battle cries or grimaces, he makes himself look ridiculous.

"There are two types of actors—the versatile one who can go from character to character, and then there is the kind who is type-cast, like Clint Eastwood, John Wayne and Charles Bronson. I see myself as lying somewhere between the two. I am a personality and each role I play shares a bit of that personality.

"I don't call the fighting in my films violence. I call it action. Any action film borders somewhere between reality and fantasy. If I were to be completely realistic, you would call me a bloody violent man. I would simply destroy my opponent by tearing him apart or ripping his guts out. I wouldn't do it so artistically. See, I have this intensity in me that the audience believes in what I do because I do believe in what I do.

"The intensity is there and I have to act in such a way as to border my action somewhere between reality and fantasy. As long as what I do is credible and as long as I have this intensity in me, then all is well.

"I didn't create this monster—all this gore in Mandarin films. It was there before I came. At least I don't spread violence. There is always justification for it. A man who has killed many people has to take the responsibility for it. What I am trying to prove is that a man living by violence dies by violence.

"But violence is there in our society. In a way I perhaps anesthetize violence by the way I move my body so that the audience calls it, not violence, but body control.

"I believe that I have a role here in Southeast Asia. The audience needs to be educated and the one to educate them has to be somebody who is responsible. We are dealing with the masses and we have to create something that will get through to them. We have to educate them step by step. We can't do it overnight. That's what I am doing right now. Whether I succeed or not remains to be seen. But I don't just *feel* committed, I *am* committed."

For this third film, Bruce refused to work with Lo Wei again. He disagreed with his methods, wanted to write his own script as well as star, and wanted a bigger cut of the profits. Lee and Raymond Chow formed Concorde Productions as equal partners to produce future projects.

"He knew he didn't have the experience to direct," says Linda Lee, "but he knew he could direct by instinct better than the directors over there."

Lo Wei had directed more than seventy-five features during thirty-five years in the film business. Almost half his films have been action flicks. He is a highly competent director by Hong Kong standards and was relatively successful with the Shaw Brothers studio before joining Raymond Chow at Golden Harvest. The problem was Bruce wanted his own way, and he wanted to use more Western production methods than seemed necessary to Lo Wei.

What upset Lee was that Lo Wei took the credit for the success of "Fists of Fury" and "The Chinese Connection" and called himself "the first million-dollar director," which was true. Because Bruce felt the credit should be solely his, there was friction between the two.

Lee's third film was "The Way of the Dragon," and

is distinguished only in that it was the first Hong Kong production ever shot on location in Europe. From a directorial point of view, it is a foolish, indulgent, rather routine film. In my opinion it is Lee's worst film.

The only redeeming features of "The Way of the Dragon" are the superb fight scenes between Lee and karate expert Chuck Norris of Los Angeles. Lee staged the fight scenes in most of his films and was good at it. His scriptwriting, attempts at comedy and general direction of the film are around home-movie quality.

The overall feel of the film is of a frivolous, light Italian comedy. Lee said he made the film only for the Hong Kong market and they ate it up. It broke all the records set on the Mandarin circuit by "The Chinese Connection."

Lee plays the role of a country bumpkin who leaves Hong Kong and goes to Rome. There he finds the lovely Nora Miao, who is running a restaurant on land coveted by Japanese and Italian gangsters. The other waiters in the restaurant are all novices at karate who follow Lee into various silly battle scenes with the mobsters.

Because Lee keeps beating the stuffing out of the gangsters, with guns or without, no matter how many the "boss" sends, Chuck Norris is imported from America to kill Lee.

The gangsters offer peace and use it as a lure to trick Lee into a trap where Norris is waiting. Somehow, from the trap, which is in the countryside, they end up fighting out the final scene on the floor of the Colosseum. Anyone who has ever been to Rome may be upset by the constant shifts in geography. For Lee, on his first trip, he could be proud of the fighting travelogue he had brought home.

If he had lived, "The Way of the Dragon" would never have been released in the United States. He knew it wasn't very good. But after his death, it was planned for distribution. According to Andre Morgan of Golden Harvest, it was to be re-edited for the U.S. audience. That means cutting the unfunny jokes and leaving in the fighting scenes. Although it was not his final film, in some places it will appear to be Lee's last effort, and it is not much of a memorial.

Even the dubbing in "The Way of the Dragon" seems inferior. Lee's voice is not actually heard in "Fists of Fury," "The Chinese Connection" or "The Way of the Dragon." In Hong Kong, actors move their lips, and words are added later in whatever language that particular print is headed for. Dubbers get about $100 per film, and a group of twenty-five people or so provide the voices for almost all the films made in Hong Kong.

The film did well in Hong Kong for many of the same reasons his earlier films had succeeded. Lee called himself Tang Lung in the film, which means "China Dragon." He went to a foreign country and proved the clear superiority of Chinese ideas and Chinese martial arts, even though he had to bend Western reality to do it.

This film does show a softer, more lovable side to Lee, which Hong Kong audiences may have found a refreshing change of pace. His cute looks and flashing eyes get plenty of play. His soft sideburns with a flip near his ear lobes give him almost a pixie quality at times.

Perhaps my real objection to the film is that Lee made half a Chinese film and half an American film, not so good as either. Instead of being camp like the first two, or exciting like "Enter the Dragon," as an American I found "The Way of the Dragon" simply indulgent and dumb. I also found the subtle Chinese comedy, which I'm told made Hong Kong audiences roar, rather bland, like won ton soup without the won tons.

The first scenes with Norris did conjure up images of gladiators. Men fighting through the twilight of a decadent civilization for the joy of their corrupt, jaded audience and masters.

Lee's version of a love story is so thin as to come off to the Western mind as nonexistent. Linda Lee says Bruce was always sorry he never got to express his sexuality more in his films. He did visit a whorehouse in "Fists of Fury" by mistake, but, as far as I recall, that was it as far as on-screen sexual relationships went. In "The Chinese Connection" Lee often seemed to be full of repressed sexual hostility. Part of the plot had him helping to keep a young girl from a life as a prostitute, and the image that came off the screen was his own sexuality bursting up from inside him like a volcano.

Certainly sex has been associated with his name. I won't even attempt to deal in this book with the accuracy of reports of his affairs, any more than I will try to disprove them. I'll only say there would have had to be three or four Bruce Lees to live all the life attributed to him.

The kung fu movies have been followed by sadomasochists as an exquisite art form. I don't think Bruce Lee ever meant them as such.

Lee's great concern now came to be new ways to stage fight scenes. He knew his Hong Kong audience was very sophisticated about fighting techniques, and he would go to extremes trying to think up new variations. Linda Lee says he would try out holds on anyone who was around, usually her, and ask how she thought it would look on the screen.

Andre Morgan of Golden Harvest recalls Bruce used to wander around the studio offices some days throwing punches and trying to work out new moves. He was a perfectionist and a master. And of anyone, he demanded the most from himself.

Bruce liked to put on head gear and spar. He would incorporate moves from boxing and wrestling that he thought fit into Jeet Kune Do. He used to say of karate practiced only by learning forms, "It's like swimming on dry land."

Bruce kept a video recorder attached to his television set in Hong Kong, as he had in California. He would tape the fights or wrestling matches and analyze every move.

"He could predict a boxer on TV was about to

throw a right hook or a left cross," says Robert Li. "Just by looking, he'd know your thoughts. He would tell students to hit and, as the thought passed through their heads, he'd know."

Another favorite stunt when he wanted to show the power sources of the body was his one-inch punch. He wanted to show the flow of energy up from the waist is more powerful in a punch than the usual shoulder-elbow combination.

"He would punch one inch from the solar plexus," recalls Linda Lee, "and send the guy flying across the room."

Bruce wanted everyone around him to be as physically aware as he was. He had the Zen "it" which he had developed over the years. It is the energy one achieves out of "oneness" and is called Ki by the Japanese, Chi by the Chinese, and closely resembles the Hindus' Prawna. Many Chinese know the power as Tao, the true life force of the universe.

In Eugene Herrigel's *Zen in the Art of Archery*, the Master tries to explain the concept to his pupil: " 'The right art,' cried the Master, 'is purposeless, aimless! The more obstinately you try to learn how to shoot the arrow for the sake of hitting the goal, the less you will succeed in the one and the further the other will recede. What stands in your way is that you have a much too willful will. You think that what you do not do yourself does not happen.'

" 'And how does one learn that?'

" 'By letting go of yourself, leaving yourself and everything yours behind you so decisively that nothing more is left of you but a purposeless tension.' "

"A true karateka (karate person)," writes Peter Urban in his fine book *The Karate Dojo*, "reaches the zenith of training when he can conquer the unyielding with the yielding. One invariably asks, 'How can a yielding object conquer an unyielding object?' This can best be illustrated by a famous karate lesson, to wit: 'There is nothing in life more yielding than a whiff of air or a drop of water, but who can withstand the force of a typhoon or a tidal wave?' The typhoon and the tidal wave are nothing more than the mass movements of air and water, which had their beginnings in a single whiff of air or a single drop of water, pliable and yielding. A karateka is relaxed, physically at ease, spiritually enlightened, but has the capability of raising himself to the heights of a raging typhoon or a towering tidal wave, sweeping away every obstacle when his life or the lives of those he loves are in danger."

There are many ways to tap the inner force once you accept it is inside us all. People with extrasensory perception tap it, as do all kinds of true mystics. Acupuncture charts trace its flow. A baseball player who learns through years of dedicated concentration to let the bat become an extension of his arm and his inner energy flow to contact the ball for hits and home runs is tapping this elusive power.

There is an institute in Japan, the Ki Society Federation, run by an aikido master named Koichi Tohei. He describes this difficult-to-understand life force as all the forces that created the universe.

"The Ki of the universe," Tohei told Black Belt, "has no beginning and no end; it can neither increase nor diminish. Though it changes its form, it remains basically unchanged.

"You and I, the sun, the moon and everything else is born from Ki. Should something made of Ki pass away, the Ki merely returns to Ki. To grasp this is to have no enemies and no allies, to know no life and no death. It is to achieve eternal, immutable life.

"You have heard of people who have picked up loads they could not have tackled under ordinary circumstances and carried them to safety in time of fire. After the fire is over, that person is unable to lift the same load. He was able to perform the seemingly impossible feat because he had instinctively unified his body and spirit during the impending disaster, while in normal circumstances his body and spirit operate independently. Should he understand the sudden superstrength thoroughly, and teach himself how to unify his body and spirit at will, he would be able to perform incredible feats in sports as well as in other endeavors.

". . . Many people forget the importance of the power of the mind and try to determine how strong a person is by his physical strength alone," wrote Tohei in his book *How to Develop Ki*, as quoted in the November 1973 *Black Belt*. "The true power of an individual can be effectively used only when his mind and body are unified."

"According to (Tohei)," continues Jon Shirota in *Black Belt*, "there are four basic rules one must first master in order to be able to execute the Ki development exercises: (1) coordinate your mind and body by settling your mind at a single spot two inches below the navel; (2) relax completely and let your strength settle down at that point; (3) lower the center of gravity of your body as low as possible so that your entire body is at the most stable and balanced position; and (4) extend the Ki so that your mind becomes one or in harmony with the spirit of the universe or nature, and your Ki becomes one with the Ki of nature."

"Through years of experimentation," writes Ed Parker in *Secrets of Chinese Karate*, "the Chinese soon discovered two types of strength—inner and outer strength . . . When referring to inner strength, this denotes hidden power that can scarcely be seen when applied, such as the breaking of twelve bricks by merely pressing the pile with the heel of the palm, and also killing a horse in the same manner."

For Bruce Lee, this inner force, what we would have called Chi, seemed almost to ooze to the surface out of his ability to concentrate his energy how and where he chose.

What separated him from other masters is that he used his Chi in great bursts as if there were no tomorrow, right up until the moment there was, for Bruce Lee, no tomorrow.

9

Enter the Dragon

"Yaakov-Yosseph took his defeat badly. He felt bitter, rejected by his colleagues, misunderstood, a victim of injustice. His friend Pinhas of Koretz did his best to comfort him with a parable: 'When the king retires at night, his crown rests on a nail fastened to the wall. Why on a nail, which is nothing but a common object? Why not on a minister's head? Because the minister might take himself seriously and believe he is the king. No such danger with a nail.'"

—Elie Wiesel,
Souls on Fire

When Bruce Lee returned from Italy after weeks of intense working and living, his original intention was to take a short rest, then start work on his next feature, "The Game of Death."

Lee knew what kind of film he had just finished. He told friends in the industry in California that while "Way of the Dragon" would be a smash in Mandarin, it would be taken as an inferior work in English.

Although Lee didn't even have a script for "The Game of Death" yet, he did have a concept. He wanted to bring a legion of the greatest fighters and athletes in the world together to costar in the film. When he got word that his old friend Big Lew, American basketball star Kareem Abdul Jabbar, was coming to Hong Kong and would be willing to work in a film with him, arrangements were quickly made. Lee and Jabbar spent a week together sparring and staging martial arts scenes for the camera.

Although Jabbar does not regularly study the martial arts, he is a natural athlete and has had a bit of instruction from time to time from Lee. At the end of their week they had some interesting footage, or at least a startling contrast.

When they were finished Lee was exhausted but plowed ahead with script preparation for "The Game of Death." Meanwhile, from among a flood of offers, things were in the final stages for a coproduction with Warner Brothers. It was this feature Lee saw as the knockout punch for the American market. The film was to be called "Enter the Dragon," and would firmly establish Bruce Lee as an international star. It did, of course, but he was no longer around to reap the rewards.

Things had been getting more and more tense in Hong Kong for Bruce. Instead of having more friends as he got more successful, he had less because he trusted fewer and fewer people. He refused to endorse friends' films, books or products, even when he thought they were good because he thought it would cheapen his image.

He was besieged with offers from producers in America, Italy and the Orient, and from independents as well. He turned down an MGM offer for a film with Elvis Presley. He had almost firmed up a deal to do a film in the future for Shaw Brothers, a costume epic, and even shot some test footage.

"It's like I'm in jail," Lee would say. "I am like the monkey in the zoo. People looking at me and things like that, and basically I like simple life and I like to joke a lot and all those things. But I cannot speak as freely as I could before because misinterpretation comes in and all kinds of things, you know.

"It hasn't changed me basically because I know that in my process of being born and going to die something happened which is breaking some records. To me, it doesn't mean anything. It's just something that happens. It's not that I'm proud or better than I ever was, I'm just the same (said with a laugh) damn old shit."

"I had a heck of a problem after my second movie became a smash," Lee told *Fighting Stars Magazine*. "I had people stop by at my door and just pass me a check for $200,000. When I asked them what it was for, they replied, 'Don't worry about it, it's just a gift to you.' I didn't even know these people, they were strangers to me.

"It was very bewildering. I didn't know whom to trust and I even grew suspicious of my old pals. I was in a period when I didn't know who was trying to take advantage of me.

"When people just pass out big money—just like that, you don't know what to think. I destroyed all those checks, but it was difficult to do because I didn't know what they were for."

Everything Bruce Lee did showed up in the Hong Kong press, and the invasion of privacy upset him. Producers would make big offers, often with little resources to back them up, and somehow it would show up in the papers. Relations between the strained star and the press deteriorated. They insisted on spelling his name "Li" no matter how often he told them it should be spelled the American way, "Lee."

Bruce wanted to be famous, but he didn't want his family overexposed by the prying cameras. It's the lament of many big stars.

His brother Peter, who still lives in Hong Kong, feels the reason Bruce got raked over so badly by the press after his death was that it was their way of repaying his refusal to cooperate while he was alive.

One night Bruce knocked the camera out of a photographer's hands because he didn't want his picture taken. " 'You've got thousands of shots,' he told them," recalls Linda, "but they took more pictures anyway."

The *China Star*, a daily in Hong Kong that goes in for short stories and large headlines, ran a multi-part series about Bruce supposedly written by one of his boyhood chums. When the fourth part came out, it so enraged Bruce he tracked down the writer and demanded to know if he had really said certain things. According to Linda Lee, the fellow told Bruce he had not said most of it. Bruce sued the paper, but no decision was made before his death. Linda has since quietly dropped the suit.

The filming of "The Game of Death" was interrupted so work could begin immediately on "Enter the Dragon," the biggest film Lee ever starred in. By American standards the budget, less than $600,000, was modest. By Hong Kong standards it was huge.

The producers of "Enter the Dragon," under the banner Sequoia Pictures, were Fred Weintraub and Paul Heller. Weintraub is remembered in New York as the one-time owner of The Bitter End, a folk nightclub in Greenwich Village. For a time he managed such personalities as Neil Diamond and Bill Cosby. He joined Warner Brothers in 1969 as a creative vice president and has overseen the creation of films like "Woodstock," "Rage" which starred George C. Scott, and "Klute" which won Jane Fonda an Oscar.

"I think every adventure film from now on will have hand-to-hand combat similar to martial arts fighting," says Weintraub, with a stroke of his salt-and-pepper Van Dyke beard. "It's a hell of a lot more exciting when it's done right than seeing a guy shoot with a gun."

Weintraub is also given part of the credit for the development of the pilot script for "Kung Fu." He had already left the project when the decision was made on a star, however.

Coproducer Paul Heller began as a set designer in summer stock and on Broadway. He moved to film as set designer and art director and for a time taught in the film school at New York University. Heller's producing credits include the innovative "David and Lisa," the thick and soupy "Secret Ceremony" which starred Elizabeth Taylor, Mia Farrow and Robert Mitchum, and Leopoldo Torre-Nilsson's "The Eaves-

dropper." Since joining Warner Brothers in 1970, he
has helped create "Dirty Harry" with Clint Eastwood
and "Skin Game" with James Garner.

"Philosophically, the kung fu films share a lot with
the American western," says Heller. "They're about
one man who has the ability to control his environment.

"In the complex society we live in there's a feeling
of helplessness against the outside world. Most people
feel they can't move against the forces around them.
And here you have the single man being able to move
and control his environment. As in the western, one
man goes and rights a wrong. I think the appeal is
much deeper than just a few films. The essence of the
Eastern philosophy involved in the karate schools, the
explosion of interest in Oriental and Eastern philosophy, the boom in Far Eastern studies all indicate this
is more than just a passing fad."

The first days' transition to the Oriental way was
difficult for many of the "Enter the Dragon" company. Weintraub and Heller arrived with a small
American crew and the other stars of the film: John
Saxon, Jim Kelly, Ahna Capri, Bob Wall, Shih Kien
and Geoffrey Weeks. Added to the cast in Hong Kong
were Angela Mao-ying, Betty Chung, Yang Sze and
hundreds of extras, some of whom were semiderelicts
to play the role of shanghaied derelicts.

First there were the climate adjustments, and almost
everyone had a touch of some kind of illness for a
while. Then a complete set had to be built from
scratch on an island in Hong Kong harbor.

Director of the film was Robert Clouse, who
received two Academy Award nominations early in
his career. Clouse was a still photographer for CBS
radio when he made his first film, "Cadillac," a short
composed of stills on film. It was nominated by the
Academy as best short subject. Another short, "Jimmy
Blue Eyes," got a similar nomination.

Clouse's first feature was "Dreams of Glass" for Universal. His only other full-length feature was "Darker
than Amber." Clouse has also written, directed and

produced for television, including two shows for Disney Productions.

Clouse told *Fighting Stars Magazine* his biggest surprise in making the film was how well Bruce Lee could act. "I'd been told, 'Bruce doesn't need to act, he's an action guy.' Well, he really surprised me. He's a good actor, as well as a supreme martial artist. And vice versa for John Saxon who we all knew was a fine actor, but who also proved to be a skilled fighter.

"You couldn't re-create that Oriental atmosphere of Hong Kong on a Hollywood sound stage for a million bucks," added Clouse. "The sights, sounds, even the smells all combined to create a feeling of intense realism for the people involved in the production. I believe that realistic quality comes across on the screen . . . I wouldn't be surprised at anything about the Orient. It holds endless mysteries and possibilities. It's truly one of the last bastions of intrigue left on Earth."

Fred Weintraub says the real mystery to him is how they ever got through the experience of making "Enter the Dragon." From the first, nothing went right, and things were ten times as hard to adjust to as expected.

"It was completely different from Hollywood," says Weintraub. "The Chinese say yes to everything, but they don't mean yes. They have no sense of the way we make pictures (in Hollywood). Their pictures have no continuity and no one cares. Instead of editing, they do their cuts in the camera (the way early silent films were done in the U.S.). They don't bother to cover each scene from a lot of angles so the editor has very little to do except string the film together."

Weintraub says they had to forget trying to record sound directly on the set because no one in the Orient is used to making sound movies so they can't be convinced to stop talking during shooting. "It was impossible to keep the crew and cast quiet," says Weintraub.

"We didn't have control of the actors," adds Weintraub. "We had a feast scene scheduled but no food. They'd say, 'Use what you have.' One day stuff was there and the next day it wasn't.

"Each actor had to be individually told what to do

in each scene. We would be trying to do a close-up of one actor in a scene of two hundred, and all two hundred would have to keep moving.

"We rented lamps, and the next day they had been returned and there were different lamps. We had to shoot everything in the scene over again. They thought the color of lamps from day to day was unimportant."

The big problem was getting actresses, recalls Weintraub. In Hong Kong, actresses are considered little better than prostitutes. "So we had to get real prostitutes to play the roles," says Weintraub. "They'd come thinking the movie business is exciting and, after six hours sitting around, they would leave and someone else would show up the next day.

"Superstition was a problem. We'd be promised a boat, and on the day it was to be used the man would tell us it wasn't a good day, the weather looked bad, and that was it, no boats that day."

The film was to have been shot in four weeks but took ten. Weintraub says he had serious problems with Bruce at first, because he demanded changes in the script to suit him.

"I was not only producer," says Weintraub, "I was first A.D. (assistant director), scene designer, schlepper. I never worked so hard in my life and was disappointed so often. Bruce was terribly nervous at first. Number two was the ego climate. When we arrived, his face was on twenty-seven magazine covers.

"Without Linda, and I really mean this, there would not have been an 'Enter the Dragon.' She kept him on a steady pace. Bruce and I were friends in Los Angeles, but in Hong Kong, we were actor and producer. Once the picture started, he was fine. It was over content, before shooting we had some differences."

One of Bruce's big complaints was his inability to agree with or work with American writer Michael Allen. Fred Weintraub moved Allen off the set to a Hong Kong hotel. Bruce got the impression Allen had been fired and reported to the local papers he had gotten the American writer removed.

Toward the end of the shooting, Bruce ran into Allen on the street in Kowloon and was extremely upset. It caused one more ugly fight with Weintraub.

Looking back on his years with Bill Cosby and Neil Diamond as they climbed toward their goal, Weintraub says, "They all change. They have to.

"He got so big, so fast, so furiously, (Bruce) was scared by it all. He had gone from obscurity to the biggest thing in the country in eight months . . . He had the minority complex as well (about being an Oriental in a Western-dominated business).

"But don't get me wrong. I'm not putting him down. Bruce was complicated, difficult, unusual. It was just amazing what Bruce had in his head. Such a vital guy."

Sets were elaborately constructed and hand-painted by teeming crews of Hong Kong carpenters and mechanics. There was a major language problem to be overcome. Not only in finding translators, who were readily available, but in finding Chinese words for English jargon and vice versa. Work began in February 1972, and shooting ran on until April.

All of the sets were constructed with hand tools and a lot of hard labor. Five hundred Chinese workmen put in numerous hours of skilled craftsmanship.

Bruce Lee staged the fighting scenes, which meant he was on the set even when he himself was not in the shot. In a scene with a cobra, Lee was bitten, but luckily the cobra had been de-venomized.

Two other serious incidents during the shooting came when Bruce Lee was challenged to a fight, and when his hands were badly cut during a scene.

There had always been lots of challenges, most often from other action actors who wanted to improve their reputation by beating The Little Dragon. Challenges were hurled at him in the street by punks and wise guys who just wanted to be able to say they fought Lee or at least got his goat. Although he was quick-tempered, Bruce usually avoided such dares.

He did get into a fight during the making of "The Chinese Connection" with one of the other actors, who had a small role, and managed him handily. Like most true martial artists, Lee felt little need to fight to prove his manhood. The beauty of the art is that it instills a maturity that lets the artist know he is beyond harm and even beyond death, so there is no need to prove himself. Most genuine Black Belts fight under only the most extreme provocation.

"On the set of 'Enter the Dragon' there were hundreds of extras, just punks," says Linda Lee. "One guy challenged Bruce. He kept hollering at him, 'I don't believe you can do everything you say you can do.' Bruce tried to ignore him, turn it into a joke. Finally he told the guy, 'I don't care what you think.'

"The guy bragged Bruce was afraid of him and refused to fight him. So Bruce, who had a bit of a hot temper as you might have heard, was just in one of those moods where he didn't feel like getting bugged. So Bruce gave him a bloody lip. The guy just kept getting up, and Bruce would say 'Enough?' He'd answer 'No.' By then, Bruce was playing with him, just playing a game . . .

"Bruce learned to turn down challenges all the time," says Linda Lee with a trace of bitterness, "and the newspapers would slam him for it. All most of the challengers ever wanted was free publicity."

Bruce rehearsed a fight scene with Bob Wall where Wall smashes a bottle and comes at him. In Hollywood the bottle would have been made out of harmless sugar. In Hong Kong it was a real bottle. Bruce thought Wall would drop the bottle at the last minute. When they ran through the scene, Wall held onto the bottle too long, and Bruce's hands were badly cut up. From a production point of view, it was a double disaster since the incident came late in shooting, and Bruce was in almost everything left to be done either as actor or fight stager.

He was finally able to return after a week.

In the film Bruce uses his own name "Lee" and plays a martial arts expert who is also an author. The plot is similar to the James Bond film, "Dr. No."

The film opens in the countryside near Hong Kong where Lee, top martial arts student of the Shaolin Temple, is met by Braithwaite (played by Geoffrey Weeks), an agent of an international intelligence organization. He asks Lee to participate in a brutal martial arts tournament on a private, sinister island fortress somewhere in international waters off Hong Kong harbor. The aim is for Lee to gain enough information to convict Han (Shih Kien), master of the island and a former Shaolin Temple student who has formed a martial arts academy to shield an international opium and white slavery operation.

Lee remembers a story told to him by an old man (Ho Lee Yan) at the temple: Three years before, at the time of Han's last tournament, five of Han's men led by O'Harra (Bob Wall) attacked Lee's sister Su Lin (Angela Mao-ying). Although she was a hapkido Black Belt, and although she put up strong resistance, Su Lin was trapped by her attackers and stabbed herself to death with a long triangle of broken glass to avoid disgrace.

Also on their way to Han's island are Roper (John Saxon), Williams (Jim Kelly) and Parsons (Peter Archer). Roper is an international rogue attending the tournament because he needs money to pay off his debt to the mob who have threatened to kill him. Williams, as he is leaving Los Angeles, is accosted by redneck police and leaves them in a heap as he takes off for the airport in their police car. Parsons, on the boat going to Han's island, asks Lee in a challenging voice what his style of fighting is. "The art of fighting without fighting," answers Lee, who then tricks Parsons into a small boat and leaves him humiliated, being towed behind the junk.

On the island the visitors are greeted by Tania (Ahna Capri), buxom mistress of the place. That evening the visitors are treated to a lavish banquet and welcomed by Han, who arrives surrounded by a bevy of beautiful female bodyguards.

Afterward Tania delivers a selection of hookers to

any of the participants who have a taste for women and Williams picks a few, Roper picks Tania, and Lee sends out for Mei Ling (Petty Chung), who has been planted on the island by Braithwaite.

That night, contrary to Han's rules, Williams takes an innocent walk around the grounds. Meanwhile Lee is taking a less innocent look and discovers below ground a huge industrial operation in which Han processes opium and keeps a large number of prisoners, including kidnapped girls he is hooking on drugs to turn them into prostitutes.

At the tournament the next day Han welcomes his "guests." After Roper and Williams easily win their matches, Han has his bodyguard Bolo (Yang Sze) brutally beat to death, with help from the mob, the four guards who let Lee prowl around the night before.

Next Lee is pitted against O'Harra, who was responsible for his sister's death and wears a scar on his cheek from Lee's father's knife slash. Although a great fighter, O'Harra is no match for Lee's lightning-fast feet and powerful punches. Infuriated by his impending defeat, O'Harra lunges at Lee with two broken bottles, but Lee kills him with a flying kick. It was this scene where Lee's hands were badly cut in rehearsal.

That afternoon Han, who believes that it was Williams who fought with the guards the night before, engages him in a fierce hand-to-hand fight. For the first time it is revealed that Han has an artificial steel hand with which he brutally defeats his opponent.

Han tries to convince Roper to join his organization as its U.S. representative, but Roper hedges when he sees the brutality of the operation. As a warning, Roper is shown Williams' body hanging impaled on a meat hook, beaten dead, above a tank of acid. As Roper watches, the gruesome body is lowered into the tank.

That night Lee re-enters the underground cavern after capturing a cobra (the one that bit him in rehearsal) left to scare away intruders. Lee succeeds in reaching the inner confines of Han's corrupt manufacturing plant and fights his way to the radio room where he sends a message to Braithwaite. Although he fights brilliantly, he is captured by Han.

In the morning's competitions Roper kills the bodyguard Bolo in a hard-fought battle, but Han's plan to have Roper and Lee fight to the death is frustrated when Roper sides with Lee. As Han sends his men after Roper and Lee, hundreds of Han's prisoners, released by Mei Ling, flood the tournament ground, and a terrific fight ensues.

While the battle rages, Lee pursues Han into a mirrored maze in which the two antagonists fight fiercely to the death. It's more a series of camera tricks than great fighting, but the effect is a powerful visual image. Leaving Han impaled on a spear, Lee returns to the tournament grounds. As he and Roper survey the remains of Han's defeated army, helicopters filled with soldiers descend upon the island.

A month before the film opened, fulfilling Bruce Lee's dream of a smash hit in the United States, he died suddenly. How he died and the theories about what killed him will be dealt with in coming chapters.

"Enter the Dragon" is his monument. It won't win any Academy Awards, because it is not the kind of film rewarded with Oscars; but, for as long as there are action films, "Enter the Dragon," because it starred Bruce Lee, will be considered a classic of the genre.

10

Mounting Problems

"When Lao Tzu died, Ch'in Shih went to mourn. He uttered three yells and departed.

"A disciple asked him, saying: 'Were you not our Master's friend?'

" 'I was,' replied Ch'in Shih.

" 'And if so, do you consider that a sufficient expression of grief at his loss?' added the disciple.

" 'I do,' said Ch'in Shih. 'I had believed him to be the man of all men, but now I know that he was not. When I went in to mourn, I found old persons weeping as if for their children, young ones wailing as if for their mothers. And for him to have gained the attachment of those people in his way, he too must have uttered words which should not have been spoken, and dropped tears which should not have been shed, thus violating eternal principles, increasing the sum of human emotion, and forgetting the source from which his own life was received. The ancients called such emotions the trammels of mortality. The Master came, because it was his time to be born; he went, because it was his time to die. For those who accept the phenomenon of birth and death in this sense, lamentation and sorrow have no place. The ancients spoke of death as of God cutting down a man suspended in the air. The fuel is consumed, but the fire may be transmitted, and we know not that it comes to an end.' "

—Chuang Tzu,
quoted from *Chinese Mystics*

The Hong Kong summer comes early with a heavy, humid hand and stays late. By the first week of May the sun was already high in the sky and the mercury high in the thermometers.

In a run-down neighborhood of Kowloon, the Crown Colony's main district, sound was being dubbed on the final print of "Enter the Dragon." Down a dusty road, among the barn-like buildings of the Golden Harvest studio, Bruce Lee worked patiently doing voice-overs for the loops of film.

The room had an air conditioner, but it was not on. Its noise could be picked up on the sensitive microphones and ruin the soundtrack. The room was like an oven, and the work became all the more difficult.

The star of "Enter the Dragon," looking tired, excused himself for a moment and went to a building next door where he closed himself into a tiny bathroom. Minutes went by as the others waited for his return in the hot dubbing room. When he hadn't returned in twenty minutes, a "gofer" was sent to fetch him.

The gofer found Lee lying on the floor semiconscious. He shook him, and the pale, sweating star rose and walked slowly back to the dubbing room to complete his work. No sooner was he back than he passed out completely losing consciousness.

A frightened stagehand ran across the parking lot and alerted Raymond Chow, Lee's producer.

"Lee had been working there the whole day," Chow told a coroner's jury in Hong Kong months later. "I asked someone to call a doctor, and I rushed into the studio.

"I saw Lee was having difficulty in breathing. He was making a loud noise and was shaking. I called Dr. Langford at the Baptist Hospital, and he told me to rush Lee to the hospital immediately."

Dr. Charles Langford, an American, was first to examine Lee upon his arrival at Baptist Hospital. He told the coroner, Egbert Tung, that Lee was suffering from high fever and was unconscious and unresponsive in the emergency room.

"Lee was brought in by several men from the studio," said Langford. "First there were breathing noises, then they stopped. There was a series of convulsions. Three other doctors were summoned, including a neurosurgeon, Dr. Peter Woo." Langford added Lee was going through muscle contraction and relaxation. "The entire body was involved in this motion, but the upper limbs gave us the most difficulty because he was very strong and was difficult to control . . . After the failure of Mr. Lee to respond for a period, and after waiting for the neurosurgeon to examine him, we gave him drugs to reduce the swelling of the brain which we had detected." The drug was mannitol.

Dr. Woo testified that Lee's eyes were moving to the right and left in a circular motion after he was revived and that his speech was slurred. He also said a blood test showed a possible malfunction of the kidney.

"It took us two and one-half hours to make Lee conscious," said Dr. Langford.

The coroner asked Dr. Langford if such symptoms would be present in a person who was suffering from overwork and exhaustion, to which Langford replied "No."

Dr. Langford said Lee was totally confused when he regained full consciousness. "It was quite dramatic," he testified. "First he was able to move a bit, then he opened his eyes, then he made some sign, but could not speak. He recognized his wife and made signs of recognition, but he could not talk. Later he was able to speak, but it was slurred, different from the usual way he talked. By the time he was transferred to another hospital, he was able to remember aloud and joke." Dr. Langford said facilities were better at St. Theresa's Hospital where Lee was taken, because there were no beds available at Baptist Hospital.

Dr. Langford said Lee seemed near death. He is also quoted in a Hong Kong newspaper as saying he "suspected that Bruce had edema (swelling of the brain) because statistics showed that Chinese have more abnormalities of brain vessels than Caucasians."

Dr. Peter Woo said he wanted to examine Lee more extensively, but the star refused. "I was going to examine the brain by injecting a radiopaque medium into it and take a series of x-rays to visualize the blood vessel," Woo said. This was done for Lee later by doctors in Los Angeles. Dr. Woo also said he had asked Lee if he had taken any drugs prior to the collapse. He says Lee told him that he had taken cannabis leaf. It was assumed this meant he chewed the leaf.

After the incident Bruce grew depressed. He flew to Los Angeles to consult with a team of medical experts. Mrs. Grace Li says when Bruce arrived in Los Angeles he told her he had come very close to death. He also told her he planned to live to be a hundred.

The Los Angeles physicians, led by Dr. David Reisbord, finally decided Bruce had suffered a grand mal, or an epileptic seizure. They said it could have been brought on by being overworked and overtired but, to be honest, they really didn't know. They did a brain scan and a brain flow study, as well as a complete physical and an EEG. Dr. Reisbord, according to evidence at the coroner's hearing later on, said he prescribed Dilantin for Lee. It's a medicine commonly given to control epilepsy. When Bruce returned to Hong Kong, he told his brother Peter the doctor had said he had the body of a twenty-year-old.

"He was in very high spirits when he came back," recalls Peter Li. "I told him I thought he looked thin. He told me he liked being thin, it made his muscles stand out more. He told me he planned to live to be a hundred."

Back in Hong Kong, Bruce began working on the final script for "Game of Death" and lining up other stars to be in it. Bruce and Raymond Chow finally settled on George Lazenby, who had played James Bond in one film, for the other major role.

While in Los Angeles, Bruce had also agreed to

return to the States in August to do an extensive promotion tour for "Enter the Dragon," including a
series of talk show appearances. He was scheduled to
appear with Johnny Carson on the "Tonight" show.

The film, it had been decided, would open August
24 at Grauman's Chinese Theater in Los Angeles amid
much fanfare. The studio felt its biggest problem was
to convince the audience "Enter the Dragon" was different from films like "Deep Thrust" and "Five Fingers
of Death" which were flooding the market. Those films
were made by Hong Kong standards, were dubbed
and consisted mostly of fighting, while "Enter the
Dragon" had Hollywood gloss, carefully smeared over
a James Bond plot using the martial arts. A natural
for the U.S. exploitation market.

As Bruce Lee became more and more famous, and
less trusting, he became warmer toward his oldest
friends, whom he saw only infrequently, yet was taking
a tougher stance about any film deals.

In Los Angeles for his checkup, Lee had had another
misunderstanding with Sterling Silliphant. Through
Lee, Silliphant had met a Vietnamese girl named
Tiana (who had a young daughter), to whom Silliphant had since become engaged. He told Bruce this
in a phone conversation and invited him to bring
Linda and have dinner with them on Saturday evening.

Silliphant says Lee told him to get rid of Tiana, that
she had two children and that he simply should not,
and could not, trust Oriental women.

Silliphant says he told Lee he knew all about her
one daughter who was, in fact, living with him. He
also knew Tiana had been Miss Karate at Jhoon
Rhee's studio in Washington. "It kind of made me
mad to find Bruce was such a (male) chauvinist," says
Silliphant.

Bruce asked how "Silent Flute" was coming along.
Silliphant told him it was going ahead at Twentieth
Century-Fox. "Who will you get to replace me?" asked
Lee. "Who could play five parts?"

"As a matter of fact, we are getting five actors to replace you, and if you were to rejoin the project, I was going to suggest that you only play one role. Playing five roles would be old Hollywood Lon Chaney stuff."

"You can't afford me anyways," Silliphant says Bruce reminded him. "I get a million dollars a picture now." They agreed to a dinner date that weekend.

On Saturday morning Silliphant says his secretary called him just as he was about to sail off for the day on his yacht and told him she had just finished a half-hour conversation with Lee. Bruce would not be having dinner with them that evening, she told him, because he didn't want to embarrass his wife by having her associate with a girl like Tiana.

Silliphant was burned and went aboard the yacht. His secretary had told him Bruce didn't really seem to disapprove of Tiana personally, but felt she had broken up Silliphant's marriage. When Silliphant told Tiana, he says she took it as an insult to her being an Oriental, and seemed to understand better than he could.

"The last time I was in Hong Kong," says Silliphant, "I met Bruce for lunch, and he had the two most beautiful Oriental girls I had ever seen with him. He said we were all set for the afternoon, but I had to leave early and go do a television interview I'd agreed to. Bruce ended up with both the chicks, and next day he said to me, 'Boy, what you missed.'

"Which goes to show the kind of curious morality of the man. What made Bruce most angry with me was that I had gone to (Japanese) karate.

"The things Bruce taught me were very valuable in street fighting, but when it comes to facing upper Brown Belts in a tournament, let alone Black Belts, I'd get killed. Absolutely slaughtered."

Bruce's arguments didn't end in Los Angeles. Back in Hong Kong he was at war with the press once more over his relationship with a Taiwanese actress named Betty Ting-pei. Bruce had first met her with Linda coming down the drive of the Regency Hyatt House in Kowloon, Hong Kong, and had since developed a friendship. Betty had a rather sordid reputation in the scandal press and was associated, truly or untruly, with all the modern ills, including free love and indiscriminate drug use.

I must say at this point, since Betty's name will come up again and again, all my efforts to reach her in Hong Kong failed. From the time of Bruce's death, she would not make herself available to the press. I was unable even to find a proper address or phone number for her.

Bruce's relationship with Raymond Chow also seems to have taken a turn for the worse. Bruce was negotiating with Shaw Brothers to do a film and, because of the rivalry between Golden Harvest and the Shaws, any participation by Chow in the project would have had to be forgotten.

Bruce's brother Peter says he was told Bruce was anxious about whether or not he was getting a fair accounting on "The Way of the Dragon" as well, although Linda Lee says Bruce never discussed such a thing with her. She says Bruce was upset with Raymond Chow because he had released "Way of the Dragon" in the Philippines before Bruce had agreed. Bruce wanted to hold off on foreign distribution for better offers.

Bruce was also angry, recalls Linda, over a story printed in one of the Golden Harvest house-written fan magazines which said Chow not only had discovered Bruce Lee but was "like a babysitter" to him.

Andre Morgan of Golden Harvest says many of the rumors were patently false and were planted in the press after Bruce Lee's death by unnamed people at Shaw Brothers studio. Run Run Shaw, of course, says that is absurd.

Lee's old difficulties with the director Lo Wei came to a head shortly before Bruce died, and again made lurid headlines.

On an afternoon in late spring 1973 Bruce was sitting in Raymond Chow's office discussing some ideas he had for fighting innovations in "Game of Death." The conversation, recalls Linda Lee, turned to Lo Wei. Bruce said he thought Lo Wei was conceited and he used people, not an uncommon trait in the film business, and something Bruce himself was often accused of.

Bruce decided he had to tell Lo Wei his feelings face to face, and upon hearing the old director was in the screening room on the lot, he walked down and began shouting at Lo Wei, who was quietly sitting with his wife. Bruce then, feeling satisfied, walked back to Chow's office.

Moments later Lo Wei's wife, who had first signed Bruce to a contract, came up to tell Bruce he should have more reserve and use more sense.

After she left, amid shouting and a gathering crowd, Bruce stormed back to the screening room and again threatened Lo Wei with physical harm and called him a string of names. Frightened, the old man called the police to control this mad martial artist, known for his temper and fighting ability.

When the police arrived, Lo Wei insisted Bruce sign a paper promising he would keep hands off. By then the whole studio was in an uproar and, Linda says, Bruce signed to end the affair. "He would have never hit an old man," she says. Bruce later told her he was angry at himself for signing such a paper, but had no other way to get the newsmen off his neck.

That night Bruce went on a Hong Kong TV talk show called "Enjoy Yourself Tonight" and, without ever mentioning Lo Wei by name, insulted him directly and indirectly. Bruce became quite heated and decided to demonstrate the power of his trick shoulder push on the interviewer. To the audience it appeared Bruce had just shoved the TV interviewer rather hard. The incident caused another wave of unhappy headlines.

For Bruce Lee, on the eve of his sudden death, the world seemed to be offering him the best and worst.

He had predicted he would be one of the world's top box-office superstars, and he seemed on the verge of accomplishing his boast. Yet the more he got, the more he needed; and the more he did, the more he had to stretch himself to do more.

"The martial arts never did for Bruce what they did for me or other people," says Sterling Silliphant. "Bruce never achieved any calm out of the martial arts. The very thing that should have protected him, didn't. He invited a lot of these slings that kept coming back at him . . . There's enough trouble in life. Most of us duck it . . . At times Bruce seemed to welcome it."

11

Bury the Dragon

"Disease can be cured; fate is incurable."

—Chinese proverb

As a guest on a Hong Kong television show one evening, on one of the Chinese channels, Bruce Lee was seated next to masters representing several various schools of martial arts. By this time Lee's Jeet Kune Do had come to be accepted by the Hong Kong public as a new school, much to the chagrin of most of the classicists.

As the show progressed, each of them told how his school of martial arts represented the ideal and why. One man in late middle age arose and took his best fighting stance and challenged each of the other panelists to push him off his stance.

One by one they got up and tried. One by one they failed. Finally only Lee remained. "C'mon, young punk," the man taunted him in Cantonese, "let's see you give a try."

Lee rose. Walked slowly over to the man in his stance. And punched him with great force in the face. The fellow not only broke his stance but fell over on his back, stunned.

Why? Why did you do it? they asked Lee.

"Because I don't push," he replied. "I punch."

It was incidents such as this that helped make Lee extremely unpopular among the men who have dedicated their entire lives and energies to a single style of martial arts, which is both their physical culture and religion.

It is such animosity that makes many wonder whether fate was alone in snatching Bruce Lee's vibrant life, or if it got a push from some secret source. I will explore the question more fully after you better understand the events surrounding his final day on earth, and the scandal that followed.

On the afternoon of July 20 (July 19 in the U.S. because of the time difference) at about one o'clock Linda Lee had kissed Bruce good-bye as she left to do some shopping. Bruce told her he had a date to meet Raymond Chow to discuss "Game of Death" and he probably would not be home for dinner.

Chow arrived and picked up Bruce. They were to go to the apartment of actress Betty Ting-pei, who was to have a role in "Game of Death," and discuss the script. Then they would all go to a restaurant and meet with Australian actor George Lazenby, who was in town to finalize his role in the film.

As best as I can reconstruct what happened from the coroner's hearing and Linda Lee's comments, once Bruce got to the apartment he complained of a headache. Betty offered him a prescription pain killer, Equagesic, which had been given her by Dr. Chu Pho-hwye, her personal physician.

Here's the *China Mail* report of Raymond Chow's testimony:

"Mr. Chow said he went to Lee's home at about two p.m. and left sometime later after working out the general outline of a script for Lee's new film, 'The Game of Death.'

"Duffy (for the Crown Council): When did you arrive at Betty Ting-pei's home?

"Chow: About four p.m. We had to finish the script before seeing Miss Ting-pei and Mr. George Lazenby.

"Duffy: How did he appear health-wise?

"Chow: Normal.

"Duffy: You had a few soft drinks?

"Chow: Yes.

"Duffy: Was he talking to you when you left at about seven-thirty?

"Chow: No.

"Duffy: When did the conversation stop?

"Chow: A few minutes before I left. Mr. Lee said that he would see me in the restaurant and then went to the bedroom. I went to the washroom and after that I left.

"Duffy: The tablet that he had taken, at what time did he take it?

"Chow: I would say about half an hour after he complained of a headache.

"Duffy: Were there any symptoms other than the headache?

"Chow: Not that I could see.

"Duffy: Apart from the tablet that he took, did you see him take anything else?

"Chow: No.

"Duffy: When did you return to Betty Ting-pei's flat?

"Chow: About nine-thirty p.m.

"Duffy: Did you look at Lee when you got to the flat?

"Chow: Yes.

"Duffy: Did he appear to be sleeping peacefully all the time, or was there any thrashing about?

"Chow: I would say that he was sleeping soundly.

"Duffy: Would there any truth to suggestions that you arrived at Miss Ting-pei's flat at three o'clock in the afternoon with Mr. Lee, and not four or five p.m.?

"Mr. Chow heatedly denied this and went on to explain that could not have been possible because they had been studying a new script.

"Mr. Chow later told the court that he tried to wake Lee by shaking him and also by slapping his face, but there was no response.

"In answer to a question, Mr. Chow said while making films Lee had, on many occasions, received blows that were not included in the scripts.

"In answer to another question, Mr. Chow said that some of these accidental blows had been quite severe."

When Chow was unable to wake Lee, Betty Ting-pei

called her physician, Dr. Chu Pho-hwye, who came right over. "When I saw Lee on the bed, he was lying peacefully, and it appeared that he had not been disturbed," the doctor is quoted as saying.

"Asked by Mr. Tisdall (Linda Lee's lawyer) why he had not sent Lee to Baptist Hospital which was a few blocks away but instead to Queen Elizabeth Hospital which was much further away, especially in view of the time factor which could have been very important in saving Lee's life, Dr. Chu replied, 'I spent at least ten minutes trying to revive him. When he did not show any signs of improvement, it did not occur to me that the time was of great importance.'"

Before Bruce's body was taken from the apartment, Betty Ting-pei's mother and younger brother arrived, apparently to try and comfort her. Raymond Chow left and broke the news to Linda Lee.

There is considerable disagreement as to what report Raymond Chow gave to the press on the night of Lee's death. Linda Lee says part of the confusion was her fault. Chow, she says, wanted to know if she had any statement to make. She says she was so upset at the time, so shocked and confused, she told him to go ahead and say Bruce died at home. Chow, a number of reporters claim, then made a statement to the press that Lee had died at home with his wife. Chow later denied he had made such a statement, when he testified at the inquest, claiming he had simply not said where Bruce died.

The first report flashed around the world, in any case, said Lee had died at home in his garden. Four days later, after a reporter noticed on an ambulance pickup slip at headquarters that Lee's body had been taken from Betty Ting-pei's and not his home, Chow said yes, that was true. The result was sensational headlines made all the more lurid by the earlier distortion, intentional or not.

Bruce Lee had two funerals, one in Hong Kong for his friends and fans, and a more private funeral when he was eventually buried in Seattle, Washington.

Between ten and twenty thousand people crowded outside the Kowloon Funeral Parlor as Linda Lee and her two children were joined by hundreds of Bruce's friends, fans and acquaintances, from his boyhood to his film career, who had come to pay their last respects. Hong Kong got its last view of Bruce Lee in an open bronze casket that cost around $40,000.

Movie stars, producers and people who had known Bruce, many weeping openly, bowed in Chinese fashion before an altar with a color portrait of Bruce. A banner, in Chinese, hung above: "A Star Sinks in the Sea of Art." Three large joss sticks and two candles burned before his picture.

On the right of the altar sat Linda, Grace Li, Peter Li and a close friend, Siu Kei-lun. Linda wore a traditional Chinese white sack for mourning over her clothes. When little Brandon and Shannon were brought in later, they put on similar white sacks and sat with their mother on a cushion on the floor. The white sacks, or robes, have been worn for thousands of years in China, where white is the traditional color of mourning. Linda wore black for the Seattle funeral.

Also in Chinese style, the funeral band struck up "Auld Lang Syne" on arrival of the mourners.

They found Bruce dressed in the same blue suit he had worn in "The Chinese Connection." The setting was also identical to that film's funeral set in which Lee had mourned the death of his teacher.

"Would you tell me what teacher died of?" Lee had asked bitterly in that scene in "The Chinese Connection."

"It was pneumonia," his fellow student had replied.

"And you believe that?"

Among the film stars attending were Nora Miao, who appeared with Bruce in "The Way of the Dragon" and who many felt had a very close personal relationship with him. Lo Wei, the director, was there. Also Nancy Kwan, star of "The World of Suzy Wong," now making films in Hong Kong. George Lazenby was there, as well as Hong Kong stars Siu Fong-fong,

Cheng Kwanmin, Cho Tat-wah, Shek Kin, Samuel Hui and Robert Chua.

Outside, a force of three hundred police held the crowd back, especially when a celebrity appeared.

The funeral in Seattle, at the Butterworth Mortuary on East Pine Street, was more sedate.

During transit, Lee's casket was mysteriously scratched, and also the blue from his suit transferred onto the white satin. The coffin had to be replaced in Seattle, which the Chinese later took to mean Bruce Lee's soul was not resting well.

Less than two dozen fans were outside the mortuary to see a hundred or so family members and friends arrive. Among those present were actors Steve McQueen and James Coburn, as well as Taky Kimura, Warner Brothers president Ted Ashley, Danny Inosantos, and of course Linda and the children, Grace Li and Robert Li.

As Bruce wished, the music wasn't traditional. There were recordings of Frank Sinatra singing "My Way," Tom Jones's "The Impossible Dream," Sergio Mendes's "Look Around," and the Blood, Sweat and Tears version of "When I Die."

Draped over Bruce's coffin was his adopted symbol, the traditional Chinese Yin-Yang symbol which represents the duality of nature and life: female-male, good-bad, light-dark, small-large, happy-sad. The Yin-Yang banner was made out of white, yellow and red flowers. Eric Lacitis of the *Seattle Times* quoted one of Bruce's students on the meaning of the symbol: "Night and day, woman and man . . . they are not opposites but are instead complementary. We say that there is a little hardness in the softness and a little softness in the hardness."

Bruce was finally buried on a grassy slope at Lake View Cemetery overlooking Lake Washington. "He lived every day as a day of discovery," eulogized Linda Lee. "His thirty-two years were full of living.

"The soul of man is an embryo in the body of man. The day of death is the day of awakening. The spirit lives on. When our day of awakening comes, we meet him again."

Ted Ashley spoke of what might have been. "It could be viewed as a pity that Bruce passed on right at the beginning of his realization that he would 'make it big.' I have a sense of sadness mingled with the realization that, while he may not have gotten up that ladder, he at least got his foot on it."

Actor James Coburn said, "Farewell, my brother. It has been an honor to share this space in time with you. As a friend and as a teacher, you have given to me, have brought my physical, spiritual and psychological selves together. Thank you. May peace be with you."

Then Coburn, McQueen, Robert Li, Taky Kimura, Danny Inosantos and Peter Chang, all pallbearers, threw their white gloves into the open grave.

Even as Bruce was being buried in Seattle, more headlines about him were appearing in the Hong Kong press. First lab tests from the autopsy, not done until thirty-six hours after death, were just coming in, and the big sensation was again "cannabis."

Eventually the fact there were traces of cannabis, or marijuana in Lee's stomach was completely discredited as a reason for his death. A doctor later said it had as much meaning as telling him Lee had drunk a cup of tea the day he died.

In Hong Kong, however, where there is almost no marijuana use, the drug conjures up images of harder drugs, much as "grass" used to be considered the "devil weed" in the United States before its usage spread in the late 1960s. Police in Hong Kong, even now, tend to pay more attention to hash or grass, it seems, than heroin or opium, simply because the substances are less familiar and have come to be associated with the dreaded "hippie tourist Europeans" (anyone in Hong Kong who is not Chinese, and who has white skin, is called a European, just as all Japanese and Chinese are lumped together in America with Vietnamese and others as Orientals).

Hong Kong police, it's said, fear local youth might discover the pleasures of grass, and what is currently a minor problem might mushroom. They quickly grabbed the "killer drug" image of cannabis and tied it to Lee as an anti-drug message. Lee's image, of course, suffered for it.

I'm going to try and make some sense for you out of the medical testimony at the coroner's hearing in Hong Kong, even though it raised as many questions as it answered. I preface the attempt by telling you the verdict eventually returned was death by "misadventure," which differs slightly from "accidental" death.

Samples of the stomach contents, urine, blood, liver, kidney, small intestine and colon of Bruce Lee were sent following his autopsy to a lab in Hong Kong where they were examined by Dr. Lam King-leung of the Forensic Division of the Government Lab. Additional samples were sent to labs in Australia and New Zealand.

Dr. Lam testified only a tiny bit of cannabis was found, about 0.5 milligram in Lee's stomach and 0.4 milligram in the small intestine. Dr. Lam said, during the tests for possible poisoning, he looked for mercury, lead, morphine, alcohol and other organic substances but did not find any. He said he could not tell if the cannabis had been chewed or smoked.

Dr. Lam also said tests showed Lee had taken drugs equivalent to one tablet of Equagesic. The doctor said Equagesic contained aspirin, meprobamate and ethohettafin, and stressed the amount found was very small. He also said that on July 24 he received four tablets, three glasses and two soft drink bottles from a detective and carried out tests on them, with negative results.

Linda Lee testified that she had first learned Bruce used cannabis occasionally after his collapse in May. She said he took excellent care of himself and would have been foolish to use cannabis more than occasionally. She said Dr. Peter Woo had warned her husband taking cannabis might be dangerous. She added Dr. David Reisbord in Los Angeles had told Lee cannabis was not harmful if taken in moderation. Dr. Reisbord gave Lee a prescription for a convulsive disorder which had to be taken three times a day, and he took it regularly. She denied Lee had epilepsy. "The word was never used and the subject was never raised by myself, Bruce Lee or Dr. Reisbord," she said.

The counsel for the insurance company asked Linda Lee if Bruce had ever used cannabis prior to his coming to Hong King. She answered, "Not to my knowledge." A $500,000 policy on Lee's life, taken out in January 1973, hinges on the question. Lee filled in a blank on the insurance company's form asking if he had ever used narcotics with a "no." If the insurance company can prove he did, they don't have to pay.

When Raymond Chow testified, there was a minor commotion after he denied he had said Bruce died at home. The reporters in the gallery and a number of spectators booed him.

Clinical pathologist Dr. R. R. Lycette of Queen Elizabeth Hospital in Hong Kong testified Lee's death could not have been caused by cannabis poisoning, but was more likely due to hypersensitivity to one of the elements of Equagesic. Dr. Lycette, who performed the autopsy on Lee, explained hypersensitivity is an adverse reaction of a body to a foreign substance. "The substance which Lee could be hypersensitive to might have been contained in Equagesic—a tablet he took—but I can't definitely say which compound in the tablet Lee was hypersensitive to," said the doctor.

Dr. Lycette explained an allergy requires some prior exposure to an agent, but hypersensitivity does not need that previous exposure. He said a person can just be hypersensitive to a substance, or hypersensitivity can be developed to a substance to which a person has been previously exposed.

On other findings of the postmortem Dr. Lycette said no injuries were found on the skull, but he found a moderate degree of congestion in the brain. Lee's brain weighed 1575 grams compared to the normal 1400 grams. "The brain was swollen like a sponge," he said. He added he had completely ruled out a brain hemorrhage because the vessels of the brain were not blocked.

He added that the back of the throat was clear and normal, and the vocal cords were free of swelling. The covering of the lungs showed some minor hemorrhaging and moderate congestion. There was some fluid in the lungs and microscopic tests showed internal congestion of the vessels. In some areas blood had burst through the vessels and entered the air space of the lungs. "There was some fluid in the lungs but no evidence of pneumonia," he said. All other organs, including the heart, were normal.

He said the brain swelling could take place within half a minute or half a day before collapse. In Lee's case, he said it developed "very rapidly."

The top expert brought in on the case was Professor R. D. Teare, the professor of forensic medicine at the University of London. He ridiculed the theory that cannabis contributed to the collapse the actor suffered May 10 or to his death on July 20. He said cannabis had been taken in various forms for centuries, and deemed it pure coincidence that shortly before the onset of Lee's collapse in May and his death he had taken cannabis.

"It would be irresponsible and irrational to ascribe the causes of death to cannabis sensitivity, if over the years there had been no previous record of such a happening," the professor stated.

Professor Teare said his opinion was that the cause of death was acute cerebral edema (brain swelling) due to hypersensitivity to either meprobamate or aspirin, or possibly the combination of the two, contained in the drug Equagesic.

Professor Teare, who was flown from London especially for this case, has been a specialist in forensic medicine for thirty-five years, during which time he has performed over ninety thousand autopsies and given evidence at eighteen thousand inquests.

Professor Teare said "misadventure" was a better word to apply to Lee's death than "accidental." He told Coroner Egbert Tung the difference was that if a man, walking alone, happened to fall and died as a result, it would be "misadventure." If he fell and died after being jostled in a crowd, then the death would be called "accidental." The difference is technical.

Linda Lee submitted a report by Dr. Ira Frank of the Department of Psychiatry, School of Medicine, at the University of California at Los Angeles that stated cannabis is not lethal. Both Dr. Lycette and Professor Teare, after study of the report and slides from Lee's autopsy, agreed.

As the days wore on, although there were police barricades set up, the crowds stopped appearing. It seemed they had come the first day to see Betty Ting-pei, but couldn't be bothered with medical testimony. By the final days only a few reporters bothered to show up at all.

12

The Midnight Mover

"Man is born with his hands clenched; he dies with his hands wide open. Entering life he desires to grasp everything; leaving the world, all that he possessed has slipped away."

—Rabbinical Ana

Martial artists who have considered the matter will tell you they do not, of course, practice killing; rather, they develop the *means* by which to kill, and that's what makes the martial arts an "art." In fact, violence is discouraged.

Yet in an art thousands of years old, with uncountable sects studying the art of killing, some martial artists could actually kill if they considered the cause just.

Indeed, there are secrets in the long history of kung fu, karate and the other forms, secret ways of killing, that live in mythology. Whenever such myths are recorded, the last paragraph often adds the art is no longer practiced, except by a few old men . . . *except . . .*

How did Bruce Lee die? He was thirty-two years old and had been told by a doctor shortly before that he had the body of a twenty-year-old. He ate only natural foods and got plenty of exercise, and his autopsy shows he was totally disease-free.

Expert evidence indicates cannabis had nothing to do with his death, which leaves the possibility that a minor pain-killing drug caused a swelling of brain tissues, and one vessel burst.

Since the swelling had occurred before, it's likely there was some other cause, natural or unnatural.

As I write this, I hear Linda Lee's voice in my head telling me to let Bruce rest in peace. The kind of speculation I am indulging in upsets her and for that I'm sorry, but I think it is worth pursuing.

Traditionally, kung fu dojos have been highly secretive, coldly cruel to those who have incurred their vengeance, and top instructors have also been experts in herbs used for healing or for poisoning.

"To graduate from a traditional . . . dojo is the most rewarding experience in a student's life. Receiving his diploma for a given grade of achievement is a thrill which a student eagerly anticipates," writes Peter Urban in *The Karate Dojo*.

"After a formal examination and evaluation, the degree master of the dojo posts great white scrolls on the dojo wall giving the names of those who have received a high enough evaluation for advancement to the next grade. In preparing for the ceremony, one readies his best uniform so that it is in perfect condition in order to make the grandest possible appearance in front of his sensei, his fellow students and the throng of visitors.

"The formal ceremonies in these dojos are a great and solemn affair . . .

"On the occasions of martial arts exhibitions in the old Orient, there was often a 'Shinken Shobu,' a fight to the death held between rival champions of different societies. They were real duels that often resulted in the death of one or both opponents. Although the British authorities put a stop to this practice in Hong Kong many years ago, it is still a frequent occurrence in isolated parts of the mainland. The jui-kumite of karate as we know it today was not practiced in the Chinese arts; their contests were never sporting events, but were always real duels. Some of the fierc-

est fights known to mankind have taken place at these
Chinese martial arts exhibitions.

"Those students," continues Urban, "who failed to
put forth their best effort at all times were often
expelled from the karate societies for a period of not
less than two years. If a student was disrespectful
toward a Japanese master or a senior dan, the most
formidable Black Belters in the dojo would take him
bodily and shave off his hair and eyebrows. They
would then throw him naked into the street where all
the students in the dojo would pelt him with stones."

Bruce Lee was among the first to display kung fu
for publicity. He put down everything the majority of
classicists stand for, and was roundly disliked for it.
Possible enemies might have been some unnamed
martial artists unhappy that an anti-establishment
karateka had such a huge public power base from
which to spread his message. And it was spreading.
Bruce Lee's Jeet Kune Do was becoming accepted as
a new sect, one that taught a form of alley fighting
that crossed the best of kung fu with American boxing
styles.

A second unfriendly group were movie and business people jealous of Lee's fame, fearful of his
power, angry over his refusal to endorse their films or
other products.

Fred Weintraub recalls a prop man in Hong Kong
who forgot to bring a prop. He felt so bad about this
"loss of face" he stayed away three days. With this
obsession for self-respect, what would a man whom
Lee had verbally or physically humiliated, or a man
whose product Lee had refused to endorse, do to get
revenge?

In the inscrutable East, there are herb poisons
Western doctors have never seen; nor could they
understand such poisons any better than they understand acupuncture.

The rivalry between Shaw Brothers and Golden
Harvest was long and bitter. Lee was changing the
face of the whole Mandarin market and had an effect

as well on much of the rest of the world. A film producer in Vietnam complained Lee's pictures were so big they had established the Hong Kong film industry as a dominant influence in Asia, putting many smaller producers out of business.

For 25 U.S. dollars, you can easily find a man in Hong Kong, one of the most overcrowded cities in the world, who will murder anyone you tell him. People Lee didn't even know hated him.

"He never sought friends," recalls Sterling Silliphant. "He was a guy who went out of his way not to make friends. He made a lot of enemies, and he didn't give a damn."

The one word I most often heard applied to Lee by those who knew him was "loner."

Linda Lee received hundreds of letters after Bruce's death blaming Betty Ting-pei, Raymond Chow, Run Run Shaw or others for her husband's death.

In California among the film colony it is fashionable to claim Lee died because he was snorting cocaine or amyl nitrite.

Ed Parker and others feel it was foul play on the part of an Oriental herbalist, although he won't even guess upon whose orders.

"Yeah, I think foul play was involved," says Parker, who has trained more policemen in martial arts than any other sensei in the United States. "Bruce was very direct, but not very tactful. You can tell a girl in a tactful way she's not very pretty, or you can call her an ugly bitch. Bruce was the direct type. He never realized she might have a beautiful sister.

"Many of us do not know the inner thinking and secrets of those herbalists in China," adds Parker rather ominously. "They have herbs for medicine and they have ones we've never heard of for poison. I believe it was foul play, but I don't think we will ever know for sure."

Parker thinks Lee might have been given a drug that would not have shown up in an autopsy performed thirty-six hours after his death.

In *Secrets of Chinese Karate* Parker describes Tien-hsüeh, or, in Cantonese, Dim Muk. "This art is the study of 'the touching of nerve points.' The study of the human system was so detailed and explicit that this system took years to perfect. Besides learning the nerve points, one also had to be skilled in reviving and administering herbs for a particular cure. This form was taught only to the most patient and peaceful members. Because of the great dangers involved, this form, which even pinpointed the effectiveness of hitting at a specific time of the day, is now becoming extinct. The few who know (and some still exist!) will take their wealth of knowledge with them to their graves."

There are some who think Japanese martial artists might have taken a hand in Lee's death. Besides the traditional Japanese-Chinese rivalry Lee always saved his special venom for Japanese karate and judo. Also Lee was the first Oriental movie star in the West who was Chinese, not Japanese.

In Japan there is a tradition of assassins known as Ninja. The Ninja practiced the art of killing, with everything from arrows to herbs, so furtively people used to believe they were invisible. In fact, their art was called Ninjtsu, which translates roughly as the "art of invisibility" or the "art of stealth."

They dressed in black from head to toe, including the face, and had concealed on the body an amazing arsenal of weapons and devices. They were geniuses at scaling impregnable walls, at the art of escape, and at killing.

They were almost egoless since they had dedicated their lives to staying safely anonymous. They were masters of disguise and totally without morals, which they referred to as "imaginary restrictions."

"Since they thrived on darkness," writes Peter Urban, "their training halls were painted completely black; varying lengths of nails and spikes protruded from the walls. Upon these spikes and stone walls, they practiced jumping, grasping, climbing and wall-scaling techniques. They were superb masters of sword-handling, archery, horsemanship, jiu-jitsu, stick fighting, body balancing, and the art of throwing tiny poisoned darts and the small, sharp-cornered coins of that era. This last was a favorite weapon, for who would believe it possible to put out a man's eye and kill him at a distance of more than fifty feet by throwing a coin the size of a silver dollar? No weapon could ever be found—just an ordinary coin 'lying in the street.' "

They were publicly banned in the seventeenth century after four hundred years of spreading terror and have since gone completely underground. Supposedly there are a few practitioners left; and in the last few years their feats have been popularized in a number of Japanese films.

"Every Ninja was an accomplished pharmacist, skilled in preparing different poisons and special powders and compounds," writes Andrew Adams in his *Ninja, the Invisible Assassins.* "Poisons were made from mineral, plant and animal sources. They were potent enough to kill, but could be weakened so that they only put the enemy to sleep, paralyzed him or made him shake with laughter. Dirks, darts and arrows were tipped with poison for assassinations. Poisons were mixed with food and drink, and even poisoned flowers were used. Curatives and medicines were concocted from herbs and shochu (unrefined sake), among other things.

"Other poisonous ingredients used by the scheming Ninja included the green rust (patina) from copper, arsenic, lycorie radiate (a type of autumn flower), buttercup and wolfbane. Swords, spears and daggers were sometimes tipped with horse dung and blood . . . The Ninja were probably the first inventors of poison gas, although it was used more as an anesthetic to put victims to sleep than to kill them. Liquid sleep potions were also devised by the busy Ninja. One involved taking hemp leaves (or cannabis), drying them in the shade and then grinding them into a powder. A liquid was made from the powder and mixed with light Japanese green tea."

An even scarier group, whose claims are almost too fantastic to believe, are Malaysians rediscovering "the art of the vibrating palm." It is an amazing technique of delayed death-striking, supposedly based on ancient kung fu practices, and employing the palm of the hand.

According to a *Black Belt* article, a Malaysian named Kah Wah Lee "has dedicated most of his adult life to studying the ancient delayed-death-strike system and its ultimate technique, the vibrating palm."

Kah Wah Lee claims it's possible to walk down the street, lay his hand on a victim, and two years later to the day (or whatever elapse of time desired), the victim will die.

"With supreme concentration, the practitioner would convert his Chi (internal energy) into resonating vibrations and transmit them through the hand to the victim's body cavity," writes *Black Belt* explaining Kah Wah Lee's theory. "The pitch of the resonance, which is apparently similar to that manufactured in the sonic breaking of glass, was determined by the desired schedule of death.

". . . Once the invading vibrations enter the body," says Kah Wah Lee, "they systematically disrupt blood flow and lung structure, the lungs being the most vulnerable of the vital organs. (Bruce Lee had strange broken blood vessels in his lungs.) Gradually, at a rate controlled by the selected time of death, the effect of the damage will increase until the body ceases to function at all. Kah Wah Lee says the initial application of the vibrating palm causes only a momentary irritation to the victim and often may go completely unnoticed.

". . . Lee claims once this vibration has been applied, it cannot be stopped, and the victim will die one, two or ten years later—whatever the assailant has selected. Consequently, a man could drop dead on a sidewalk while his murderer is sipping tea with friends on the other side of town."

Then there are the Shaolin monks. Caine on the "Kung Fu" TV series is supposed to have been trained by them. Bruce Lee was supposedly defending their honor when he brought down Han in "Enter the Dragon."

The legend of the Shaolin monks goes back almost as far as the history of the martial arts itself.

"About fourteen hundred years ago (between 500 and 600 A.D.), Daruma (Bodhidharma), the founder of Zen Buddhism, left Western India, penetrating mountain ranges including the Himalayas and crossing unbridged rivers through complete wilderness, to travel to China to present lectures on Buddhism," wrote the late Gichin Funakoshi, who introduced karate to Japan, in his masterwork *Karate-Dō Kyōhan*. ". . . In later years, as he traveled to the Shaolin Temple in Hunan Province in China to lecture there on Buddhism, a great multitude of followers fell one by one in exhaustion from the harshness of his training. Daruma then set forth a method of developing the mind and body, telling them, 'Although the way of Buddha is preached for the soul, the body and soul are inseparable . . . For this reason, I shall give you a method by which you can develop your physical strength enough to enable yourselves to attain the essence of Buddha.' . . . With it, the monks were able to recover their spiritual and physical strength, and it is said that these monks of the Shaolin Temple came to be known throughout China for their courage and fortitude."

The principles of kung fu developed there were based on imitation of animals. The index finger knuckle protruding out of a fist is the "eye of a phoenix," while the middle finger knuckle protruding is "the dragon's head." Other hand positions are based on the eagle, the crab and the tiger.

From that temple spread the message of weaponless fighting art, carried by some of the toughest men ever to don a monk's habit.

At that time China was run like one big family, and each citizen had to do as father government ordered. The only way to break out of the family was to become a monk, thus in essence becoming part of God's bigger family. This meant only monks were free to roam, and in those times wanderers had to be tough. Few were tougher than the Shaolin monks.

According to legend, the monastery had three gates—front, rear and side. Any man desiring to be a monk entered through the rear gate. Anyone kicked out or allowed to quit also used the rear gate. Those monks who were there to pray but not fight used the side gate. The front gate was hardly ever used.

Did you ever notice the dragon tattoos on Caine's arms in "Kung Fu"? He would have gotten them, had he been a real monk, going out the front gate.

Once a man entered, he began years of fanatical physical and spiritual training (especially physical). He had to pass three tests to "graduate" out the front gate. The first test was on his knowledge of the oral tradition. The second test was in combat against his instructors and fellow students. The third test required him to take a short walk down a deadly hall of horrors to prove his ability, instincts and guts; or die trying.

The candidate, without hints or warnings, "was led through the monastery cellars to a labyrinth built far beneath," writes Peter Urban in *The Karate Dojo*. "Once he was inside, the doors would be closed and sealed, preventing retreat. The candiate knew there was only one way out: his fate would be either triumph or death. The labyrinth, which was divided into two chambers, was cold and damp; the walls oozed moisture and were slimy to the touch. Rats, spiders and reptiles brushed against, clung to, and scurried around the candidate. There was almost total darkness; there were pits that had to be instinctively avoided, for one false step would be injurious if not fatal. Arrows and spears shot out from concealed hiding places in the walls. Stones and axes fell without warning and had to be dodged or caught. Eerie shadows danced in the shallow light which fell on the skeletons of former, unfortunate candidates, who now served as ghastly inspirations."

"If the student successfully survived his trip through the hallway," writes Ed Parker in his *Secrets of Chinese Karate*, "the last and final test was to move a 500-pound urn that was red hot, in order to allow his freedom through the last doorway. The manner in which he had to move this urn was by using his forearms to hug it, thus branding his forearms with two symbols—one of a dragon and one of a tiger. This, then, was the diploma of a Shaolin graduate of Southern China. Wherever he went, these symbols brought him respect and honor."

The Shaolin monks even scared the authorities. Eventually they were attacked by government armies, but instead of fighting, they scattered throughout Southern China to teach and rebuild.

Who knows? If the descendants of these monks were upset with Bruce Lee for any of the many reasons previously mentioned, it was within their power to do him evil.

"Secret societies have played an important role in Chinese history from earliest times," writes Bruce A. Haines in *Karate's History and Traditions*; "however, the first outspokenly anti-government group existed near the end of the Han dynasty, called the 'Carnation Eyebrow Rebels.' Because of the effectiveness of this society in accomplishing its aims, the list of such organizations grew until eventually whenever political oppression became intolerable, or a foreign power came to rule (such as the Mongols of Marco Polo's time), these secret societies led the fight in restoring desirable government.

". . . In every true art form, whether esthetic or practical, some part of the artist's technique is kept secret. This is especially true of Chinese (kung fu).

Even at the present time, ancient (kung fu) is kept in relative secrecy among the physical culture clubs that practice this art. In the past five years in the United States, (kung fu) secrecy and selectivity have appeared to diminish somewhat, so that whereas before only those of pure Chinese ancestry were accepted as students, now all racial groups can be found studying the art. However, upon closer scrutiny, it can be seen that many techniques normally included in (kung fu) are excluded from the open teachings, and are taught to those of Chinese ancestry at a different time or in a separate location.

"The 20th Century, far from witnessing the demise of (kung fu) has seen a great rise in its popularity. In Communist China, Mao Tse-tung has utilized the appeal of (kung fu) to enlist participants in his gymnastic program, as well as for a pragmatic form of self-defense that everyone is urged to learn. Numerous Chinese 'boxing' magazines are printed in Red China and Hong Kong, with thousands of readers found throughout the Chinese communities of the world.

". . . Though it appears that kung fu . . . is becoming a universal art along with the other karate-like styles of self-defense, it is possible that we will never see it practiced as it once was in the fabled temples of Shaolin."

So there are many secret ways Bruce Lee might have been done in. It would have taken only one talented enemy who had the knowledge and the will, and Bruce Lee had many enemies on many levels of the martial arts.

Lee was the midnight mover. He arrived quickly, struck suddenly and died without warning. Was his fate tampered with? We will probably never know. He did leave us with a legacy, though, not only for his growing son, but for everyone who believes there are secrets in the East worth unlocking. Bruce Lee made himself both loved and hated by being among the first to unlock the secrets for more than a few Chinese.

"Well, I can tell you one thing," Bruce Lee said. "Like any art, ultimately the martial arts are self-knowledge in the sense that a punch or kick is not so much to knock the hell out of the guy in front of you, but to knock the hell out of your ego, your fear, or whatever hang-up you have. Because once that is clear, then you can express yourself freely."

13

The Boom from Angela Mao's Room

"The walls of a city are raised by men's wisdom, but
overthrown by women's subtlety."
"As in the Yangtze waves push waves, so in the world
new men replace the old."

—Chinese proverbs

Can you name a film actress whose recent film got a
standing ovation at the Cannes Film Festival, who
has ten feature roles to her credit, but has never
heard of Fellini, Goddard or Mike Nichols?

Can you name an actress with a worldwide reputation who has earned her studio millions without ever
exposing even a naked shoulder?

Can you name an actress who is scheduled to star
in four full-color feature films per year, all the flicks
expected to be big money-makers, who will make less
than $10,000 per year for her troubles, and who lives
in a modest four-room flat?

The answer to all these riddles is Angela Mao-ying,
known in the U.S. simply as Angela Mao, a slender,
childlike woman in her early twenties, best known for
her deadly on-screen hapkido antics.

In the past several years Angela has been starred in
such films as "Deep Thrust," "Lady Kung Fu" and
"Hap Ki Do." She was also featured as Bruce Lee's
sister in Warner Brothers' "Enter the Dragon."

For all her efforts, Angela collects lumps and
bruises, fan mail from around the globe, and a paltry
$150 per week from her studio, Raymond Chow's
Golden Harvest Ltd. of Hong Kong. She has no say

over her scripts, no power to choose her director. Under a five-year contract she signed when she was twenty, she must work whenever and on whatever films the studio assigns her. She is a voluntary vassal in the far-gone tradition of the late, great Hollywood. But even Zanuck and DeMille would have been awed by the control an Oriental film studio exercises over its contract players.

I interviewed Angela in the Hong Kong office of Golden Harvest through an interpreter provided by the studio. While the interpreter was a lovely young lady, she kept referring to the studio as "our company" and interpreting Angela's answers as the studio would deem best. If there are any gaps in the interview, I choose to blame them on this language barrier.

Although her films have girdled the globe, recently exploding in popularity, Angela's horizons are almost entirely limited to Hong Kong where she now lives and works, and Taiwan where she grew up.

She was amazed when I told her how popular her films were all over the world, including Europe, the Arab countries, and America where "Deep Thrust" grossed $4 million. By the way, when Angela made that film it was called "Lady Whirlwind." She had not heard the title "Deep Thrust," which was applied by Hallmark Films in Boston, until I mentioned it to her. Even then, she was a little baffled by the several translations we tried.

Off the set Angela wears almost no makeup and only rarely visits a hairdresser, yet she radiates grace and femininity. She complains that people tell her she looks like a man on screen, but mostly because she plays tough, uncompromising, almost masculine roles, karate-chopping any brute who raises her temperature to vengeance.

She has clear coffee-brown eyes and blemish-free white-bronze skin. Her shiny black hair falls short of her collar in an easy shag. Among her ruby nails the only jewelry are too small rings, one with her boyfriend's initials, which she bought herself.

Angela's boyfriend, whom she says she recently became un-engaged from, is eighteen years her senior. His name is Kelly Lei Chun; he was a lead actor in the early Sixties, but now suffers from headaches and some sort of blood disease. He apparently has recovered sufficiently to go back to work in an off-camera capacity at Golden Harvest; and Angela told a Hong Kong paper just before I left that her parents were no longer against her romance with Kelly. Angela glossed over the subject with me, and I got the impression her romance was on the downswing.

Angela says she doesn't socialize much, likes to stay at home with a few friends, and spends most of her spare time on hapkido, her martial art. Unlike Bruce Lee, she not only believes in a system, but readily puts down all other martial arts by comparison.

Angela began studying Korean hapkido during her first film, a forgettable epic called "The Angry River" that was never released outside the Mandarin film circuit.

She has since become a real martial artist, studying hapkido as both physical culture and way of life. She opened a fan magazine which featured her in a frightening pose on the cover to proudly show me a picture of her sensei (instructor) on the second page. Her first and only director, except for American Robert Clouse on "Enter the Dragon," insisted during the filming of "The Angry River" that she begin studying the martial arts, and she has been dedicated ever since.

She has been dedicated to her director, Huang Feng, ever since as well. She told me, as if it were quite common, that under her Golden Harvest contract she has no other director, unless the studio loans her out, as in the case of "Enter the Dragon."

Angela's scene in "Dragon," while short, was one of the strongest in the film, I thought. She is Bruce Lee's sister in a flashback. She is walking with their father when they are attacked by bullies. The old man tries to defend Angela, slashes O'Harra the leader across the face (played by American martial arts expert Bob Wall), and is knocked down. Angela runs off, with the gang in hot pursuit. Each time they corner her, she uses her considerable skills to kick the hell out of them and run off again. Finally they trap her in an old warehouse. She saves her virtue by picking up a long triangle of glass and, with a dramatic grimace, convincingly commits suicide in sort of Japanese hara-kari fashion.

Angela wasn't a newcomer to show business when she began in films. In fact, at age twenty, she already had fifteen years' experience behind her. She began playing roles in the Opera on Taiwan when she was five, as part of her school training. She even went on a world tour that included her only visit to the United States, when she was twelve.

Her appearances in the Opera were part of her reward for being a standout pupil at the Foo Hing School, which is well known in Taiwan and Hong Kong for its specialized teaching of all the traditional Chinese arts. Angela, who says she has little interest anymore in music, Chinese classical or otherwise, has given up her singing for acting.

The school was residential and provided a tightly disciplined, well-chaperoned upbringing in traditional Chinese principles. Angela lived at the school from age five to thirteen, when she rejoined her parents. Angela's father was also a performer in the Opera, although, like Bruce Lee and his Opera-star father, they never performed together. Angela was the third of seven children in her family.

In 1969 a mutual friend introduced Angela to director Huang Feng, who sized up her potential immediately. He inked her to a no-loophole contract for 3000 Hong Kong dollars per month, which equals about 600 U.S. dollars. She also gets a four-room flat in the company apartment building, but has no say in the content, quality or shooting of her scripts, or who costars or directs. Likewise, she has no say over budgets, locations or crew. There are no craft unions, aside from house unions, in the Hong Kong film industry; and fringe benefits, like insurance, private studio cars and resident personal makeup people or hairdressers, are unknown.

Angela says she has sustained at least minor injuries during every one of her strenuous film roles. Several years ago she was hospitalized for sixteen days after her back was severely strained filming a kung fu leap in "The Thunderbolts," unreleased in the West.

All of Angela's films have featured her using hapkido, although she says she would like to try some variety, particularly a love story. She says she does not feel she has made any fine films yet, but came closest in a melodramatic tragedy called "Back Alley Princess," likewise unreleased in the West.

Asked about Women's Liberation, she looks dumbfounded. After repeated questioning she finally says, yes, she has heard there is such a movement, but she has no interest in it. She agrees men and women should be treated as equals, but the question is of no relevance to her life.

As she fumbles for an answer and our interpreter discusses the point with her in Cantonese, I suddenly realize where I am. Just outside the window, women with pickaxes are doing street construction, and a few miles away others are literally pulling a plow. Liberation isn't very important to women, it seems, where even the men aren't very liberated yet. Anyway, in China, men and women have always shared the work, if not the wealth. In Mao's China and in Chiang's Taiwan, women hold positions of power and are accorded quite important places in society.

Liberation, Angela aptly points out, is a matter of necessity. It is unnecessary for her to trouble herself with it, she explains.

Angela says she would like to direct films herself in the future if she stays in the movie business. She has a fatal attitude about it, knowing the kung fu chop-socky flick era will pass, and feeling she will probably pass with it. She talks vaguely about going into some kind of business, but has no firm ideas. "The arts life," she says simply, "is limited."

She giggles when questioned about marriage. She says it doesn't interest her right now, but that eventually she would like to be married and have three children.

Angela has modest tastes and, for Hong Kong's number one starlet, modest ambitions. Her attitude seems to be to let her busy schedule simply live itself out and let the future work itself out.

Fashions don't turn Angela's head either. She has no complaints about an income that won't finance trips to salons in Paris or Rome, because she has only a small wardrobe and picks things that will inter-match the same way any working girl must.

During our interview she wore a practical brown patterned sweater and slightly faded brown bell-bottom dungarees. She might have been a girl sitting next to me in class at UCLA or NYU or even the Sorbonne. In most of her films she is seen attired in a white gi, the baggy martial arts uniform, with the hapkido symbol, an eagle clutching an arrow, on her chest. Another favorite outfit is baggy jacket and trousers in a patterned material cut like traditional Chinese pants suits.

The pretty girl with the sparkling eyes also tells me she avoids parties and larger dinners, preferring an evening at home with a few friends. She goes to the movies when she has time, including her own films, and says Marlon Brando is her favorite Western actor. She has not seen "The Godfather" or "Last Tango in Paris." In fact, she has only a vague notion that "Last Tango," which was banned by Hong Kong censors, even exists.

She has no political interests and supports establishments everywhere. She lives by the Buddhist code of moderation and believes good gets as good does.

Angela loves to read love novels and watch soccer matches. Her favorite participatory sports, after hapkido, are basketball and bowling. Tennis, like Fellini, simply is not part of her world.

Among Oriental actors Angela expresses the greatest respect for Bruce Lee who, she says, treated her like a sister. Lee once coached her in a film to help her improve her on-screen kung fu techniques. Lee asked that his name not be associated with the film, but his picture appears in all the advertising, even though he is never seen in the film.

She says Bruce Lee's advice to her was, "A person cannot forget someone who is good to them."

While she says she knows she is a Virgo, born September 20, 1950, she doesn't credit astrology with much accuracy. It is about half right, half wrong, in a general sort of way, she says.

When questioned about grass or stronger drugs, another puzzled expression crosses her ivory face. Again, drugs are simply something she not only hasn't tried, but has never even considered.

Would Angela do a nude scene? Absolutely not, she says. She tells me with a stern expression director Robert Clouse tried to get her to allow her shirt to be ripped off by the gangsters in "Enter the Dragon," but she refused. Then he asked her to allow her sleeve to be ripped at the shoulder for dramatic effect, exposing only her smallpox vaccination, but she refused. In most of her films she is covered in a tunic and baggy pants from head to toe.

Angela says she would like to do a film in Hollywood for the experience, but doesn't think it will ever happen because she speaks only Cantonese. She expresses embarrassment several times during the interview about her inability to speak English.

Angela says she would do a love scene, tastefully, but anticipates being embarrassed by it when the time comes. She doesn't feel her films are overly violent, even though censors around the world have disagreed. Her films, and all the chop-socky films, have been severely treated by censors, particularly in Great Britain, complains producer Raymond Chow.

Angela's answer to demands from Singapore, Taiwan and other places to cut excessive violence is to eliminate the gushing blood, not the action.

Do chop-socky flicks contribute to crime in the streets? The question brings a complex non-answer, concluding with the thought that there is no possible relationship, in her opinion. Angela does admit some of her fans imitate her, but suggests that is not such a bad thing.

In fact, Angela vocally recommends other women take up hapkido as a hobby because it will keep them trim, provide healthy exercise and teach them self-defense.

How have the martial arts changed her life? Her only reply is that her physical reactions are much quicker now.

Angela Mao-ying seems to realize she is being exploited by her studio, but it is of little real matter. Her contractual relation with Golden Harvest is a traditional Chinese way of doing business. She is not just an employee, but a member of the company's family. Few Hollywood veterans of ten feature films, all of which were financial bonanzas, would still have such a glow of freshness and innocence.

For years people have been astounded by the salaries and egos of American film superstars. Perhaps, Angela proves, if the salaries had been less, the egos might have been less; but exploitation is quite another matter. The studio is making big bucks with Angela's kicks and chops, and she deserves a larger share, yet her sweetness is refreshing.

Angela says she still gets a thrill out of being recognized by her fans on the street because it represents a measure of success. Her rewards up to now certainly haven't been financial, but she has an inner calm and radiates a warm beauty.

On screen Angela has done in scores of men with a brutality most women can hardly even fantasize. Off-screen she has hardly been involved with one or two.

An unpolished gem, she is worth far more than she herself realizes, but the men who sell celluloid and popcorn have done very well cashing in on the frail girl who gets her kicks out of the martial arts.

14

Instant History

"Bruce Lee really did a lot for the martial arts. Anytime somebody does something on television in a worthy way, that automatically gives it a lift. Recently there was a 'kung fu' movie on television. I'll tell ya, I had hundreds of calls because of that. I signed up maybe a hundred students just because of that."

—Aaron Banks,
New York City dojo
operator and karate
tournament promoter

Perhaps in some far future time when karate is taught in every high school, as it once was on Okinawa, and the *I Ching* is as much an executive's tool as his pocket calculator, Bruce Lee will be a footnote in the history books. If so, he will be remembered as the man who broke East-West barriers on the screen and arrived with proof of the theory that East is moving West and West is moving East.

Lee was both a sign of his times and a portent of the future. If Mao hadn't rebuilt China, if Nixon hadn't gone to Peking, or if the Hong Kong film industry hadn't gone through a shakeup, Bruce Lee might well have gone unnoticed, or been confined to the Mandarin film circuit at best. Instead Lee exploded on the world scene, from Beirut to Honolulu, with the suddenness of a firecracker. He became the first Chinese-American superstar.

While the martial arts are still generally misunderstood in the West, he made them harder to ignore.

The body of films he left behind aren't full of great drama or artful acting, but they are head and shoulders above almost everything else in the "kung fu" genre, and must inevitably be regarded as classics of their kind.

No idea, philosophy or religion ever takes hold in a culture without being changed itself. If the martial arts time has come, and at least three hundred thousand Americans who study the subject believe it has, then it must change to suit new needs, just as karate adapted to customs and needs in its trip from China to Okinawa to Japan.

Perhaps Bruce Lee's greatest contribution ultimately will be judged to have been his attempt to create a new Western martial arts based on simplicity, directness and non-classical performance. He leaves us no guidebook on kata (form) or manual of instructions on adapting kung fu to the Western culture, just the notion.

"Let it be understood once and for all that I have *not* invented a new style, composite or modification," Lee wrote in *Black Belt* explaining Jeet Kune Do in September 1971. "I have in no way set Jeet Kune Do within a distinct form governed by laws that distinguish it from 'this' style or 'that' method. On the contrary, I hope to free my comrades from bondage to styles, patterns and doctrines."

Consider part of the message Bruce Lee bore, although he often failed to live up to it himself. It entails a world based on omens, mutual physical and mental prowess, a society of respectable elders and respectful youth. A world without styles or dogma that divide people. Instant retribution. Instant karma, based on years of laborious training and moral philosophy. Complete near-religious dedication. And perhaps a world without guns or other arms. A world of weaponless self-defense, in place of the cannons and bombs that have proved nothing in world wars, added nothing to the world and destroyed much.

Lee was a hero you could believe in. He didn't fight on screen out of lust, just good old blood revenge. Offend his sister and he will smash your head. He was a brother, he was a muscle for a movement whose time is approaching.

Then again perhaps history has already passed by weaponless combat in this nuclear age, and kung fu is just a fad like nostalgia or "Superman" reruns. Film distributors say the Chinese boxing films have dropped off disastrously at the box office, and the last of them may very well hit the theaters by the first anniversary of Bruce Lee's death.

Yet gladiator films will always be popular in some form, and martial arts combat is truly exciting to watch on the screen.

The dazzling cartoon-like ultra-violence of the martial arts movies, or chop-socky movies as the trade paper *Variety* calls them, holds a strong appeal for kids like Tatum O'Neal weaned on the instant images of television; and sometime in the future those images are likely to be translated into actions that could reflect a new life style.

"Martial arts films will change," predicts producer Fred Weintraub, "just as, say, Douglas Fairbanks was the first of the swordsman kind of thing. After him came more. Martial arts films of the Chinese genre have seen their best days. I mean, you will not get away with cheaply made films just because they have martial arts. There is such a vibrant reaction to ("Enter the Dragon") I can hardly believe it.

"Remember," adds Weintraub, "in Hong Kong, there were thirty films playing. All of a sudden a guy named Bruce Lee played in half a film ("Fists of Fury") and suddenly this guy nobody knew was a star. This picture with somebody nobody knew did $750,000 (3.5 million Hong Kong dollars) which meant practically every single person in Hong Kong —the most densely populated city in the world—had gone to see the film.

"It's like when Clint Eastwood emerged as a western star. All of a sudden guys began coming out of the woodwork. It may take two or three years, but all of a sudden some guy will capture the imagination of the public. I think Bruce's going to be a legend."

"It's my feeling now that Bruce Lee will become a James Dean figure of the Seventies," writes folksinger Phil Ochs in the music publication *Zoo World.* "James Dean was a great actor finishing three films before dying in a car crash at age twenty-four. Bruce Lee was not that kind of actor, but on a physical level he will survive in the imagination as long as there are movies. They both found their way into mythology by a brief, but totally magical, presence on the screen followed by a sudden and meaningless death."

The cloud over the Bruce Lee memory is the shock of his sudden death still weighing heavily on those whose lives he touched. And truthfully, he was a complex human being, an eccentric genius in his occupation, who made friends and fans, but who also made legions of enemies who cannot forget their hurts.

Sportswriter Jim Murray used to call champion American football coach Vince Lombardi "White Fang" because he could be completely charming one moment and turn on you with startling viciousness the next, instinctively probing your most tender weakness. So it was with Bruce Lee, who at times seemed to believe he was perfect, who demanded impossible perfection in others, and who imperfectly died when his mission seemingly had just begun.

The comment I have heard most often from my under-thirty friends, who go to a lot of action films, is that one man with a gun could have ended most of the martial arts films in three minutes, bang, bang, boom.

In Hong Kong and Singapore, where there are practically no guns in any hands except those of the police (following the British tradition), and in other parts of Asia where many people simply can't afford or find access to guns, men fighting with their bodies, swords and other traditional tools seemed quite realistic. In Hong Kong, fans are experts on fight scenes and care little about plots. In the Western world many action fans forgave the lack of plot, but not the lack of guns in the frontier tradition.

The second comment I have heard is, if Lee was such a superman, a health nut and trained continuously, why did he die at the age of thirty-two? There is no answer. That's why wild theories about various foul ways Lee might have been done in take on so much credibility. It's simply unbelievable such a vital man could have slumped over suddenly of natural causes.

The chop-socky films, taken without any understanding of the martial arts, are pure cinematic violence, and many people worry about how mentally healthy it is to sit through two hours of bloody action. I know some people, mostly women, who will not go to any film that has screen violence in appreciable amount. The films also lack a certain charm for distributors who feel they will be difficult to market to television after their theater run for this very reason, too much violence.

"I don't think (the boom in martial arts) is just a fad," says sensei Ed Parker, who has a vested interest, "because the need for self-defense is growing. It is no longer a luxury, it is a necessity. There was a long time when people wanted physical security, then we got it. For a long time since people have wanted financial security. Now we have gotten financial security, and we are reverting to a need for physical security. A lot of people see what Bruce could do with his hands and feet, and they identify. They want to do it, too. Martial arts movies have brought a lot of people in to study, without a doubt."

In the Orient the martial arts are part of the way of life. Yet Lee's biggest box-office smash, "Enter the Dragon," in its Chinese language version, did not do well in Hong Kong. The reasons are complex.

Bruce Lee understood the cinematic needs of the Eastern and Western market: different audience

tastes demand different products for each. He felt
"The Way of the Dragon" would not be accepted in
the West, although it broke box-office records in the
Orient, and he probably would not have been surprised to hear Hong Kong audiences found "Enter
the Dragon" unrealistic and glossy and felt the fighting scenes were inferior. The things about the film I
heard mentioned often in Hong Kong were the girls'
blowing darts out of their hands with incredible accuracy, and the final fight scene between Han and Lee.
Others felt Lee should have been the one to defeat
Bolo, Han's top fighter, and not Roper, a Westerner.

Another observer, a Chinese who has lived in both
Hong Kong and the U.S., says the Chinese were angry
at Lee, whom they had come to look upon as an
international hero and spokesman, for dying and
leaving them adrift, leaderless. "He's already dead,"
they'd say. "What's the point?"

There was also a great deal of anger toward Raymond Chow, Lee's producer, who had distribution
rights to "Enter the Dragon" on the Mandarin circuit.
It was felt he exploited Lee's death by raising admis-
sion prices from 5 to 8 Hong Kong dollars ($1.60
U.S.). Chow says the price was set before Lee died.
There was also animosity toward Chow over the
claim that he had lied about where Lee died in the
first statements. Some Chinese complained "Enter the
Dragon" was released all over the globe before being
released in Hong Kong, and this is generally true.

All the bad publicity and scandal headlines surrounding Lee's death did not help the film much
either. Lee was associated with sex (being found for
whatever reason in Betty's apartment) and drugs (all
the discussion of cannabis). His status as a hero had
been turned into a national joke. Anytime someone
tried a martial arts stunt, they were taunted with lines
like, "Hey, who do you think you are, Bruce Lee?"
His name has taken on extra meanings that have
turned it into a symbol of ridicule in many cases.

As Andre Morgan of Golden Harvest points out,
the film didn't really do badly, just not as well as

expected. It grossed about 3.5 million Hong Kong dollars, or about 750,000 U.S. dollars. That's about the same as "Fists of Fury" grossed when it broke box-office records two years earlier.

On the other hand, Hong Kong isn't the universe. Fred Weintraub says "Enter the Dragon" has exceeded all expectations in many places around the world. It recently displaced "Diamonds Are Forever" as the box-office champ of the Philippines. Weintraub says Warner's expects worldwide rentals to exceed $18 million (now add television rights for a rip-roaring success).

Bruce kept telling Weintraub during the filming of "Dragon" that the thing that would make him happiest would be if their film outgrossed Steve McQueen's "The Getaway," then also in production. Weintraub says if he could send Lee a telegram in heaven, it would read " 'Dragon' outgrossed 'Getaway' everywhere."

Edward Stokes, director of advertising for Hallmark Films in Boston, has had the job of overseeing exploitation and promotion of many of the kung fu films, although none of Bruce Lee's. His company is responsible for importing such films as "Deep Thrust" with Angela Mao, "Karado: The Hong Kong Cat," and "Shanghai Killers." He says the films, from a purely profit-picture viewpoint, have done best in black areas of big cities and in drive-ins. He says they generally did better west of the Mississippi than east of it, although the place they did best of all was very east, New York City. The other best towns were Chicago, San Francisco and Philadelphia. If a city had a big Chinatown, business was better, he noted.

"There have been so-called cycles before," says Stokes, "but those were maybe two in one year. Here we have everybody in on the act all at once. This thing is lasting about two years, and at first we didn't think it would last the summer. Remember, in New York City, there have been as many as thirty of these playing at one time."

Stokes compares the films to operas and says most

people see the action not as violence but as a kind of joke that turns it into escapism. He compares the plots to an opera where the heroine sings for thirty minutes at the end during her death scene. "In the kung fu pictures," says Stokes, "the guy dies for thirty minutes. You can't help but be entertained."

Stokes says the Chinese-made films eventually will fail because life styles are just too different for people to identify with. He says Lee was accepted and his name remembered because he had been on television in the States and had done various kinds of promotions. Stokes says it has been almost impossible for him to get audience recognition out of the name "Karado," which he thought was going to be a natural. In fact, American audiences (more than Europeans) seem to have difficulty remembering any Chinese names.

Criticism of Stokes and Hallmark comes from reviewers who bitterly complain they can't properly write about, and thus publicize, the chop-socky flicks because often the only thing they are told about them is the title. (On American films, critics get thick press books that quite often show up in print as their own thoughts. I say that admitting I, too, am a film critic.)

"Latest crop of martial arts features from Chinese producers picked up for U.S. distribution," wrote *Variety* in October 1973, "may be bringing some box-office happiness to exploitation exhibs, but they're being treated like garbage by distribs and critics in New York. Scribes (newspapermen) are grumbling about the few pix screened for review (they wish there were fewer) and most indies don't bother to screen pix at all. Lack of respect for the genre is rampant, except at the b.o. (box office), and even that may be seeing the light at the end of the tunnel.

"Latest example is 'The Screaming Tiger,' an American International pickup, which was screened here last week. AIP continues its policy of screening all of its releases, but in this case the policy was cursory.

"Critics present at the showing were handed a

reprint of pic's newspaper ad with title, copyline ('The scream of the tiger is the cry of revenge'), name of lead actor (Wang Yu) and MPAA rating (R). That was it. No producer, director, cast, etc. No running time, no nothing. Projectionist was to time the film at the screening and give that info to departing scribes.

"An AIP touter was on hand to take the complaints from those who publish full credits with reviews (like *Variety*) and to jot down the credit list off the print and thus belatedly provide it. Pen in hand, he watched with amazement when print started to unspool. Except for the title, all credits were in Chinese."

"I don't think anybody was too interested in getting reviewed," answered Stokes. "Most reviewers don't write for the 'kung fu' market."

Stokes says in the future, to succeed, martial arts films must be better made and have a gimmick. Black martial arts, sexy martial arts, or martial arts well integrated into an interesting plot will be successful. Hallmark, by the way, has already stopped buying foreign-made martial arts flicks for the American market and intended to release the last of those in its bins by mid-1974.

Only Golden Harvest in Hong Kong continues to make and believe in Chinese boxing films. "Kung fu has established itself," says Andre Morgan, Raymond Chow's top assistant at Golden Harvest. "I think there will always be a place for kung fu action in movies. I don't think the market will accept crap anymore, though."

Fred Weintraub says he would never make another film in Hong Kong under the same conditions as when he and Paul Heller produced "Enter the Dragon." He says he learned his lesson and on more recent films they have taken almost an entire crew with them on location.

Yet the Hong Kong film industry certainly has matured out of the Bruce Lee explosion. In a single year a twenty-year-old industry has seen its first international star, done its first location shooting, and begun its first truly international coproductions (the Shaws previously were involved in coproductions with Japanese and Taiwanese producers).

Weintraub also says, given another two or three years, he believes Bruce Lee could have lived up to his boast that he would be the biggest box-office attraction in the world, bigger than Charles Bronson or Steve McQueen.

"If you could have taken five films from 1971 to 1976," says Weintraub, "and line up the box-office takes of Bronson, McQueen, Paul Newman, Robert Redford and Bruce Lee, outside the U.S., I would bet Bruce Lee would have come out on top."

Bruce Lee leaves us with this note, written only two months before he died, when he heard Taky Kimura had recently split up with his wife. ". . . In life," he wrote to Taky, "there are the pluses and the minuses, and it is time for you to concentrate on the pluses. It might be difficult but fortunately for us human beings, we have self-will. Well, it is time to employ it. Life is an ever-flowing process and somewhere on the path some unpleasant things will pop up—It might leave a scar, but then life is flowing on and like running water, when it stops, it grows stale. Go bravely on, my friend, because each experience teaches us a lesson, and remember, if there is anything at all I can help with, let me know. Keep blasting because James Lee did, and life is such that sometimes it is nice and sometimes it is not."

As surely as East is moving West, and West is moving East, Bruce Lee lives.

15

Author's Confessions

"Flood, fire and robbery only hurt the body, but heresy injures the soul."

—Chinese proverb

There is one more theory about how Bruce Lee died we need to explore. There are those who say he made the gods jealous, and jealous ancestors are angry spirits, who might have stolen his thunder back.

Lee believed in his destiny and was moved by powerful forces. One physician in Hong Kong who studied the case concluded Lee had a birth defect, a defective cell that sat like a time bomb in his skull; and that single cell simply burst on July 20, 1973.

Every artist believes he has a fireball inside himself and, at his best, he taps this elusive energy and marshals the force for his creative end. We have seen this energy defined as Ki or Chi and know it is normally tapped by martial artists through discipline, patience and obedience to ritual. Lee tapped it as though the raw energy of the universe were his personal property to parcel out at will. He was bigger than life, and big targets are felled first.

I believe in this final theory because I think it was the inborn imperfection of Lee that both drove him to fame and killed him. He simply stretched himself out like a canvas more and more taut until a single pinprick popped him into eternity.

Since much of this book has been filled with personal observations, you may have been wondering who I am and how I came to write this book. I have never formally studied the martial arts and never met Bruce Lee face to face, although we had one phone conversation long-distance between Ocean Beach, New York, and Kowloon, Hong Kong.

I first heard of him while doing an article for *Crawdaddy* on the explosion of interest in martial arts. A short time later, while discussing article possibilities with an editor at *Esquire*, I mentioned Lee, and of all my ideas submitted, that was the one they accepted.

They authorized a story on Lee and guaranteed that, even if it was not printed, if I finished it they would pay me a minimum for my troubles, or what is known in the trade as a "kill fee."

I wrote the article under difficult circumstances and, due to a number of factors, *Esquire* turned it down and paid me the "kill fee." Several months later they called me back, shortly after the release of "The Chinese Connection," and asked for another look. The second time they printed it as part of a group of martial arts stories in the August 1973 issue. The magazine cover was white, the Chinese color of death, and Bruce Lee died almost the same week the article appeared on the newsstands.

At the end of the *Esquire* story there was a cartoon filler, unrelated to my story, which pictured a mother cat on a street depositing two kittens into a wire basket marked *Put Litter Here*.

On the day Bruce Lee died (July 20 in Hong Kong and July 19 in the States due to time changes) my cat Ram Bam gave birth to three kittens, two of whom died.

By that point I felt my karma irrevocably interwoven with Lee's, and I knew I had to continue my search. I followed the case in the press and through various sources wrote a newspaper series for the New York Times Special Features syndicate that became the basis of this book.

I took leave from my job as entertainment editor of the *Miami News* and in less than six weeks traveled over twenty-six thousand miles, talked to dozens of people, read a shelf full of books and wrote these words. If they have faults and gaps, as I know they do, it is because I wanted to cover as much as I could as quickly as I could.

On November 27, 1973, which is Bruce Lee's birthday, I stood in the cold rain with Taky Kimura and said a prayer at Bruce Lee's grave in Seattle. At that moment, three thousand miles away, my cat Ram Bam, staying with my (honestly) Aunt Lee, gave birth to her second litter of three more kittens.

As Bruce Lee knew, it was his destiny to live as he did. I know it was my destiny to record his feats in my own way, and this book was born in that spirit.

Some people have asked me how I can write about death, but I have tried to explain throughout this book that I am writing about a new life, in fact, an ancient life force finding new converts.

While the first wave of martial arts films is fading, the martial arts are here in the Western world to stay. Kung fu in movies and on television is certainly not going to disappear. More likely, there will be better films which integrate the physical side of kung fu with the spiritual side and wrap both in interesting plots and dialogue. Such films will do well.

Who will some of the stars of tomorrow be? As Fred Weintraub has pointed out, there is no one, at the moment, with the same screen vitality as Bruce Lee. Probably no one will ever be able to replace him. But after the settling-out process, in a few years, others will rise to be nearly as important, just as knowledgeable, although perhaps in different ways.

Most television and film executives in America still have little understanding of the real martial arts. Like children fascinated by the phony superjumps of stuntmen in Chinese boxing pictures, many executives see only the violence on the surface and are incapable of looking beyond it.

In 1972 during a press conference I asked Fred Silverman, a vice president in charge of picking which programs go on the CBS television network, if CBS was developing any programs involving the martial arts to compete with the superpopular "Kung Fu" series on ABC. Silverman answered with a curt put-down, telling me "we" didn't need any more of that kind of "violence" on television. CBS, by the way, then proceeded to fill their season line-up with hour after hour of phony detectives and lawyers. *U.S. News & World Report* says, in fact, a study found the average TV viewer saw violence depicted in eight out of every ten programs and nine out of every ten cartoons during the 1972–1973 TV season. And most of that violence wasn't "revenge," it was simple dumb-crook-kills-and-smart-cop-catches nonsense.

There were a number of films set for 1974 release that feature kung fu, and I will mention some of them, and the stars. Many involving the martial arts were aimed toward the so-called black exploitation market.

Fred Weintraub and Paul Heller have starred Jim Kelly in a modest production called "Black Belt Jones." Kelly had a small role in "Enter the Dragon," and is also due to be seen in an Allied Artists film, "Three the Hard Way" with Fred Williamson and Jim Brown.

Kelly is a talented natural athlete who, until he began acting, had made his biggest splash as a star of the karate tournament circut.

Kelly, who is baseball star Willie Mays's cousin, starred in football, baseball and track while in high school. He is reputed to have long-jumped 21 feet 1 inch when fifteen years old. He led his high school conference in scoring for three straight years at Bourbon County High in Kentucky.

After high school Kelly accepted a football scholarship to the University of Louisville, but the first of his many "attitude problems" began to haunt him. After only two days he became disenchanted and, outside of playing frosh football, liked nothing about the school. It was in Kentucky that Kelly first began studying Shorin-ryu karate, later switching to Okinawa-te karate.

After quiting Louisville, Kelly, always a smart dresser on screen or off, headed for California where he talked himself into a football scholarship at San Diego State the following season. Two days before classes began, upset by a family dispute, Kelly again bolted, this time moving to Chicago and leaving his football career (and bright prospects for an NFL career) behind.

In 1968 while working for an airline Kelly began making his mark on the karate tourney circuit. By 1971, when he won four championships in a row, he was a star. Only problem with the professional karate circuit is it doesn't pay enough to live. Kelly was interviewed for an article in *Black Belt* titled "A Trophy Can't Put Gas in My Car."

To live, Kelly taught karate, did some modeling and continued improving his martial arts techniques. While his movie career now looks promising, he told me in a brief interview he doesn't foresee himself staying in films indefinitely, although he isn't sure what else he wants to do.

Kelly's costar in "Three the Hard Way" is Fred Williamson, who also stars in "That Man Bolt," featuring the martial arts.

Williamson, a six-foot-three-inch, two-hundred-ten-pound former pro football player, was also seen in "The Legend of Nigger Charlie." During his career with the Kansas City Chiefs he had begun studying aikido off-season because he says it kept him in excellent shape.

In "That Man Bolt," shot mostly on location in Kowloon, Hong Kong, Williamson plays Jefferson Lincoln Bolt, a courier assigned to transport a million dollars from Hong Kong to Mexico City via Los Angeles, under difficult conditions.

"The battle sequences," according to a Universal studio press release, "consist of about ninety percent karate. If ardent practitioners of the martial arts look close enough, they will also see some kung fu, judo and aikido. Oriental weaponry highlights some of the duel sequences; in one scene Williamson, under attack, rolls off a bed and with a lightning-fast throw, nails the assailant in the chest with a shuriken (knife-like object with a handle). Other weapons used in fight scenes are chukkas (a round piece of wood with a one-inch rope used chiefly by swinging at an adversary) and tonfas (a long stick with a handle—sometimes used as protection against chukkas). In addition to Oriental weapons, hand guns are used throughout the film."

"Three the Hard Way" is the story of how three black superstuds come together to save New York City from a plot in which whites are murdering blacks by poisoning the water supply. With a budget of almost $2 million and Gordon Parks, Jr., directing, it is one of the biggest-budget features with martial arts yet done.

One of the first films featuring martial arts to be a success is on its *n*th run. That, of course, is the phenomenal "Billy Jack," which is now expected to gross $60 million. This idealistic little film centers on a school on an Indian reservation in the southwestern United States. Billy Jack is an Indian who was trained in the martial arts in the Armed Forces, and who serves as a one-man police force on the reservation against white poachers.

While the success of "Billy Jack" is due to a number of factors, everyone involved has been quoted as saying the use of martial arts was definitely a part of the box-office draw.

The most important film upcoming from Golden Harvest in Hong Kong is currently titled "When Twe Kwan Do Strikes," but will get another title for the American market. It stars Angela Mao and Jhoon Rhee, a Korean martial artist who owns a chain of dojos in the Washington, D.C., area.

Also coming from Golden Harvest is "The Chinese Professionals," featuring nine men from around the Orient, each with a fighting specialty, who come together when hired as mercenaries by a martial arts school. The director is Wang Yu, and the star is Wang

Yu. Who is Wang Yu? He is another former Shaw Brothers star who walked out on his contract in a dispute over pay and joined Raymond Chow's Golden Harvest. His split got heavy publicity all over the Orient, and Shaw openly denounced Wang Yu in the press. Two of the other "professionals" are pictured as Tibetan llamas who are masters of the Mi Chung technique, which supposedly means they can control their circulation and close off pressure points voluntarily, thus rendering themselves invulnerable to those Oriental fighting techniques which kill or maim their victims by attacking these pressure points. Thai kick boxing, which many believe is the most commercially viable of all martial arts as a spectator sport, is also seen in the film.

Another film is the troubled "Karado: The Hong Kong Cat." Troubled at the box office, that is, where Hallmark, the distributors, can't figure out how to get American audiences to identify with their dynamic hero. The *Los Angeles Times* called this the best martial arts film since "Enter the Dragon": "Cheung (who is Cheung Nick, the star who plays Karado) hardly has Lee's animal magnetism, but he sure can move. Dubbing is better than usual, gore-letting is low for the genre and, for once, we have a coherent wild-East story."

The plots of "Triple Irons," "Sacred Knives of Vengeance," "Cobra Knows No Mercy," "Queen Boxer," and "Fists of the Double-K" all revolve around revenge. All involve martial arts. And all will fascinate action freaks and turn off those who feel any violence on screen is to be avoided.

I'll be watching for the success or failure of these films, and perhaps the grand ancestor of all martial arts films, Bruce Lee, will be watching from his mountain outpost far away, too.

A Final Note

"O.K. Honorable Master Kung Fu! I accept your daring
no-risk free-trial offer to reveal the secrets of KUNG-
FU! Ship in plain wrapper at once. I enclose $3.98
as payment in full. I understand that there is nothing
else to buy ever again. My friends and I must be delighted with my new KUNG FU! power and self-
confidence—or my money will be refunded promptly
in full . . ."
—From an ad in *Official Karate Magazine*

I cannot end without some warning to any reader
who is inspired by this book to go out and study the
martial arts. Kung fu rip-offs are widespread. There
are many instructors unqualified to teach and many
con artists who set up karate or kung fu studios, accept
advance payments and disappear.

Before you begin studying the martial arts, find out
all you can about your instructor. Anyone who has not
had five to fifteen years previous training is unqualified
to teach others on his own. Do not sign any contracts
for lessons. A reputable instructor will usually need no
such guarantee.

Con men have been known to come into an American town, rent a store front, put out a sign reading
"Karate," and begin signing up pupils. They ask you
to sign a contract for ten or more lessons which is
really a promise to a loan company that you will pay
a certain amount. Then the instructor factors off the
contracts, meaning he sells them to the loan company
for a portion of the money, and leaves town. You are

still legally obligated to pay even though you get nary a lesson.

Also, I am sorry to say, beware of any instructor who got all his training in the Armed Services, especially one of the Vietnam camps. Often pupils were passed up to Black Belt almost automatically so their instructor's service records would not be marred.

Traditionally the best dojos have not even advertised. If you want to study, seek out someone you know who is already studying, several people if possible, and ask for guidance. These days there are reputable schools which go in for advertising, but extreme caution should be taken.

Finally, understand that the martial arts may not be learned quickly. It is a hard discipline that comes with years of repetitious training and sweat. No reputable instructor will promise you quick or easy results. Better than half of all beginning students, it is estimated, drop out within a few lessons because they cannot take the physical training. But after six months or two years or however long it takes, there comes a new awareness of your inner Chi that will make it all worthwhile.

As for me, I've found my karma through Bruce Lee and I'm off to find my dojo.

Bibliography

The books listed below, by author or primary editor, were the principal sources (aside from original interviews) used in "The Legend of Bruce Lee." Among periodicals we express special thanks to *Black Belt*, *Karate Illustrated*, and *Fighting Stars* magazines. We also referred during our research to *Professional Karate* and *Official Karate* magazines.

Black Belt, Karate Illustrated, 20th Century Warriors, Los Angeles: Ohara Publications, Inc., 1971.

CHEN, JOHN T. S., *1001 Chinese Sayings*, Hong Kong: Chung Chi College, 1973.

COWIE, PETER, *International Film Guide, 1973*, New York: A. S. Barnes & Co., 1972.

DHIEGH, KHIGH ALX, *The Eleventh Wing*, Los Angeles: Nash Publish., 1973.

FUNAKOSHI, GICHIN, *Karate-Dō Kyōhan*, Tokyo, New York, and San Francisco: Kodansha International Ltd., 1973.

HAINES, BRUCE A., *Karate's History and Traditions*, Rutland, Vermont, and Tokyo: Charles E. Tuttle Co., 1968.

HUA, ELLEN KEI, *Kung Fu Meditations*, Ventura, Calif.: Farout Press Books, 1973.

HUMPHREYS, CHRISTMAS, *The Wisdom of Buddhism*, New York: Harper & Row, 1960.

KWONG, Y. T., and T. C. LAI, *Chinese Proverbs*, Hong Kong: Kelly & Walsh, Ltd., 1970.

LEGGE, JAMES, *I Ching, Book of Changes*, New York: Bantam Books, 1969.

LIU, DA, *T'ai Chi Ch'uan And I Ching*, New York: Harper & Row, 1972.

PARKER, ED, *Secrets of Chinese Karate*, Englewood Cliffs, N.J.: Prentice-Hall, 1963.

SIU, R. G. H., *The Portable Dragon*, Cambridge, Mass.: The MIT Press, 1968.

TZU, LAO, *The Way of Life* (translated by Witter Bynner), New York: Capricorn Books, 1962.

VAN OVER, RAYMOND, *Chinese Mystics*, New York: Harper & Row, 1973.

WESTBROOK, A., and RATTI, O. J., *Aikido And The Dynamic Sphere*, Rutland, Vermont, and Tokyo: Charles E. Tuttle, Co., 1970.

A day in the lives of a city's police:

Robert Daley

Target Blue

A patrolman stares at the Mayor as His Honor bends over the hospital bed where an ambushed policeman lies dying. A "cool" Police Commissioner turns ice cold with rage when he hears the full extent of corruption among his men. A bearded detective with torn clothes and an ear ring stakes out a pusher. Another plainclothesman in an expensive suit and using a French accent waits for a beautiful hooker to put the make on him. A patrol car in a ghetto is surrounded by a mob howling for blood. The most respected man on the Force is ordered to hand in his resignation.

An Insider's View of the N.Y.P.D.

ROBERT DALEY SPENT OVER 365 DAYS LIKE THAT WITH THE NEW YORK POLICE DEPARTMENT IN A POSITION WHERE HE COULD SEE THE TOTAL PICTURE, FROM BOTTOM TO TOP. THAT WAS AS MUCH AS HE COULD TAKE. NOW HE HAS WRITTEN A BOOK THAT FOR THE FIRST TIME GIVES THE FULL STORY.

A Dell Book $1.75

THE TAKING OF PELHAM ONE TWO THREE

a novel by
John Godey

If you cannot obtain copies of this title from your local bookseller, just send the price (plus 25¢ per copy for handling and postage) to Dell Books, Post Office Box 1000, Pinebrook, N. J. 07058.

MIKE SHAYNE MYSTERIES
by Brett Halliday

More than 30 million Mike Shayne mysteries have been printed in Dell Book editions alone!

ARMED . . . DANGEROUS . . . 60c

THE CARELESS CORPSE 75c

CAUGHT DEAD 75c

FIT TO KILL 60c

GUILTY AS HELL 60c

THE HOMICIDAL VIRGIN 75c

I COME TO KILL YOU 60c

KILL ALL THE YOUNG GIRLS 75c

MERMAID ON THE ROCKS 60c

MURDER IN HASTE 60c

MURDER SPINS THE WHEEL 60c

NEVER KILL A CLIENT 75c

PAY OFF IN BLOOD 75c

A REDHEAD FOR MIKE SHAYNE 75c

SHOOT TO KILL 75c

SO LUSH, SO DEADLY 60c

If you cannot obtain copies of these titles from your local bookseller, just send the price (plus 25c per copy for handling and postage) to Dell Books, Post Office Box 1000, Pinebrook, N. J. 07058.

"unusual, gripping and menacing"
—*New York Times*

SHOOT

by DOUGLAS FAIRBAIRN

"This is what happened. Myself and four friends were hunting along the Stirrup River one weekend in the deer season . . . when we noticed that there was another party of deer hunters standing on the opposite bank . . . Then, all of a sudden, without any warning and I swear to God without any provocation from us, one of them raised his rifle and fired, hitting Pete Rinaldi in the head . . ."

From that spare beginning, this gripping tale of violence moves through the unfulfilled lives of its small-town war veterans, their sex-entanglements and gun fantasies, to a full-scale mini-war.

"Like James Dickey's superb novel, *"Deliverance,"* 'SHOOT' is about the American male's quest for manhood through violence and sex."

—*Tuscaloosa News*

"A tough, fast-moving chiller right up to the terrible climax."

—*Jackson Daily News*

A DELL BOOK $1.50
Soon to be a major Columbia movie

HOW MANY OF THESE DELL BESTSELLERS HAVE YOU READ?

1. **THE TAKING OF PELHAM ONE TWO THREE**
   by John Godey $1.75

2. **A DAY NO PIGS WOULD DIE**
   by Robert Newton Peck $1.25

3. **QUEEN VICTORIA** by Cecil Woodham-Smith $1.75

4. **ELEPHANTS CAN REMEMBER**
   by Agatha Christie $1.25

5. **TREVAYNE** by Jonathan Ryder $1.50

6. **RAMBLING ROSE** by Calder Willingham $1.50

7. **THE MAN WHO LOVED CAT DANCING**
   by Marilyn Durham $1.75

8. **MEAT ON THE HOOF** by Gary Shaw $1.50

9. **SOLDIER** by Anthony B. Herbert $1.75

10. **11 HARROWHOUSE** by Gerald A. Browne $1.50

11. **THE CAR THIEF** by Theodore Weesner $1.50

12. **THE GREAT EXECUTIVE DREAM**
    by Robert Heller $1.75

13. **TARGET BLUE** by Robert Daley $1.75

14. **THE GLOW OF MORNING**
    by Irving A. Greenfield $1.50

If you cannot obtain copies of these titles from your local bookseller, just send the price (plus 25c per copy for handling and postage) to Dell Books, Post Office Box 1000, Pinebrook, N. J. 07058.